# PMP Prep Exam

# 2023 – 2024

The Essential Guide to Acing the PMP Exam, which includes the latest updates, Practice Questions, and Detailed Solutions

Willie P Howard

**ISBN:** 9798871537114

# DEDICATION

To all who embrace live as a gift

# TABLE OF CONTENT

# Chapter 1: Introduction To Project Manager

## What is project management?

Project management involves the application of methods, techniques, abilities, expertise, and experience toward accomplishing particular project objectives within the stipulated period. It entails assigning and managing the human and financial resources of a company to advance a particular project, event, or responsibility. Project management can refer to a one-time project or a continuous activity, and resources managed consist of persons, technology, funds, and intellectual property. The ultimate outcomes of project management are subject to financial and temporal limitations. Project managers often have the same duties regardless of the industry: they assist in defining the project's objectives and purposes and decide who is responsible for completing each component at what time. They also establish quality control procedures to guarantee that finished parts fulfill a predetermined level of quality. To summarize, there are five steps in the project management process: planning, initiating, executing, monitoring, and closure.

## Example of Project Management

Suppose a project manager is given a task to oversee a group of workers who are building a production plant. His first step is to identify the project's scope. Next, he assigns the team with specific tasks, which could be made up of quality assurance specialists, engineers, developers, and construction planners. He also sets deadlines and a timetable for the project.

In order to keep track of the exact activities to be performed by which departments, project managers frequently utilize visual workflow representations like Gantt charts or PERT charts. They create a budget that has enough money in it to cover unforeseen expenses and still keep the project on schedule. For the team to carry out their duties effectively, the project manager also ensures that the necessary resources are available.

When a bigger firm buys off a smaller firm, an essential aspect of the project manager's role is to bring together project team members from different backgrounds and develop a sense of common goals for attaining the final goal. Although they may possess some technical expertise, project managers also have the crucial responsibility of taking high-level corporate visions and producing concrete results on schedule and within budget.

## What Do You Understand As A Project?

A project can be described as a series of tasks that are expected to be completed within the stipulated period, or, simply put, a project is a mix of fixed objectives to be fulfilled within a set amount of time. It also involves a set of inputs and outputs needed to accomplish a specific objective. Project management is an excellent way of organizing both your business and non-business objectives. Changes made during the project completion phase are expected to improve performance. Working on a project for school or college requires cooperating with other students to achieve the goal. Moreover, working on an office project also requires all parties involved to come together for the success of the project. Even when you are working on your personal project, you will have to coordinate between workers, friends, and family to achieve the goals. Therefore, even if a project is owned by an individual, it requires a collective effort to complete the project. These individuals are referred to as project managers. Projects can be basic or complex, and they can be handled by a single individual or a hundred.

## Characteristics Of A Project

**Projects are unique**

According to the PMBOK Guide, projects are only temporary and initiated with the intention of producing a unique service or goal. Each project is unique and distinct from any other due to its own purpose, goals, location, structure, resources, activities, and other project characteristics.

A project is a single entity.

Although a project brings together people with different kinds of skills, colors, participants, and even disciplines, that does not exclude it from being a single entity. Without denying the fact that it combines all its components, it still remains a single entity.

**Cross-Departmental Collaboration is Required for Projects**

Teams or individuals with diverse roles, responsibilities, and skill sets from different departments must work together on projects in order to accomplish a shared goal or find a solution. In project management, collaboration is extremely beneficial since it brings together the critical knowledge, abilities, and ideas needed to produce results.

Projects are Vehicles for Experiencing the Unknown

There is some risk and uncertainty involved with any project. This is because, until an activity is actually carried out, very little is known about its outcome throughout the project life cycle. Projections of results are, therefore, typically the foundation of programs.

However, the amount of risk varies from project to project. This will depend on a variety of factors, including the resources available, the toolset chosen to carry out the project, and how successfully the project is planned and guided through the phases of the project life cycle.

## Projects Have a Goal

A project is defined by the Project Management Institute (PMI) as a collection of human and non-human resources used in a short-term endeavor to accomplish a particular goal.

Initiatives are started with the goal of achieving particular goals in relation to the resources at hand. A project will come to an end once its goal has been accomplished. The conclusions that have been reached are recorded for future reference. Monitoring and assessment are carried out as the project moves through the predetermined phases to make sure that its goals and reasons for being are met.

## The Nature of a Project

A project is optimistic in nature. Every project manager hopes that the purpose and objective of setting up a project will be met and that the end result will improve the initiator of the project. Projects differ in terms of their size, industry, goals, structure, and results.

All projects, no matter how big or small, must nevertheless go through an anticipated life cycle from the beginning to the completion.

### The Project Life Cycle

The project life cycle, also known as a project process, consists of five primary phases. It makes more sense to divide a project into phases for efficient execution and monitoring, considering the amount of labor involved in planning a project from start to finish. The project life cycle offers a structure that enables the project's resources and activities to be arranged logically to maximize resource use and, ultimately, produce the greatest results.

### Every project phase has specific objectives and will comprise:

A list of tasks that must be completed during the phase
The duties and details of the team members
Project outcomes.
Resources allotted for that particular project phase
Guidelines for performance monitoring

### The stages involved in the project life cycle

A project's life cycle is further divided into phases.

### Project Initiation Phase

Projects begin with the project initiation phase. A project is usually launched to respond to an opportunity that demands to be explored or an issue that requires a solution. A cost-benefit study ought to have been completed by then.

To complete a cost-benefit analysis, you must have conducted a feasibility study, project scope definition, deliverables, and stakeholder identification to come up with a business case. This stage delineates:

The company's goals and objectives

Project objectives and the benefits they will provide to the company

An inventory of all the project's stakeholders

Project outcomes.

Project budget and scope

Concerned hazards

Once each of the above details has been validated and the project has been accepted, the project formally begins, project teams are formed, and planning commences.


**Project Planning Phase**

Given that the planning phase influences the project's vulnerability and outcomes, the planning phase is the most important one for any project. The project manager must understand the goals and needs of the project before initiating any planning.

The planning phase is where the project plan is drawn to give directions to all stakeholders. It lists every job, activity, responsibility, expense, schedule, deliverable, milestone, and other dependency needed to complete the project effectively.

The project plan is essential for carrying out, overseeing, and completing the project since it outlines the aims and objectives of the undertaking as well as the "who gets what and does what" and "how to" of implementation.

**Documents provided during the planning phase:**

Scope statement

The Work breakdown structure (WBS)

The Project Plan

The Project Schedule

Change request management

Communication plan

Project quality plan

Acceptance plan

**Project Execution Phase**

The execution phase usually takes the longest and requires the largest amount of resources when the project is completed. Two of the most important stages in accomplishing a project's objectives are project planning and execution. This is the point when it becomes really important to manage the project's resources, keep an eye on its development, and ensure that all parties involved are communicating clearly.

To carry out the tasks listed in the project plan, the project team makes use of the WBS and the project schedule. He provides periodic status reports to ensure that all the stakeholders are kept abreast of the project's progress.

The Project manager conducts regular team meetings to discuss change requests, assess project deviations, report project progress, and revise the project plan as needed.

Communication should follow the guidelines outlined in the communication plan.

The project is prepared for closure shortly after the deliverables have been created, the final product is presented, and the customer has approved it following the acceptance criteria.

**Monitoring and Controlling Phase**
While monitoring and control are meant to serve as checks on every step of the project management process, they are more useful in the execution stage. Ensuring that the project proceeds according to plan and stays within its allocated scope requires monitoring and control. The risk is reduced when the project moves forward according to schedule.

Monitoring the project's current progress should ideally be contrasted with the anticipated performance and the proper action to be taken in case of a deviation.

**Closing Phase**
This final stage, sometimes referred to as the follow-up phase, is when the teams and the project manager gather together for a closing meeting to go over the project's developments and insights. Once the project's objectives have been met and the final result is prepared for distribution to the client, it is closed. For future reference, they will compile a summary of the full life cycle, highlight its lessons and takeaways, pinpoint its advantages and disadvantages, and record it with other project data.

## When Do We Use Project Management?

Projects are distinct from routine business operations and take place when a company needs to provide a solution to specific needs within a specified spending limit and time frame. When you need to achieve a certain demand, it makes sense to use project management. Projects necessitate the temporary gathering of a team to concentrate on particular project goals. For initiatives to be successful, excellent teamwork is therefore essential. One purpose of project management includes ability to manage according to a set of requirements.

Projects necessitate the temporary gathering of a team to concentrate on particular project goals. For initiatives to be successful, strong teamwork is therefore essential. Discrete work packages are managed in project management in order to accomplish predetermined goals. Many different aspects affect how the work is carried out.The scope, importance, and difficulty of the task are evident; while moving a small office and planning the Olympics present many of the same fundamental management difficulties, they also present quite distinct ones.

## When And Why Do We Need Project Management?

One cannot overstate the vital role of project management in businesses. When done correctly, it facilitates the smooth operation of the entire company.

The goal of PM is to create a final product that is beneficial to the organization that initiated the project by bringing about some change. To produce this final result, several tasks must be planned, initiated, and controlled. It frees up your team from the interruptions brought on by projects going off course or out-of-control spending to concentrate on the job that really matters.

Formal management is necessary for projects that:

Possess a limited duration with a clear beginning and finish.

Create something fresh, modified, material, or immaterial.

The task at hand involves intricate work or multiple organizations.

Call for risk management

Change management is required.

**Investing in successful project management will yield several advantages, including:**

increasing the possibility of getting the intended outcome
guaranteeing effective and economical resource utilization
meeting the various demands of the project's participants

## Who makes use of the project management?

The process of applying skills, techniques, and resources to
successfully finish projects is known as project management. Even
those who aren't formally referred to as "project managers" handle
projects. Project management techniques are widely used by
businesses in a variety of sectors, including manufacturing,
construction, and technology. A certain amount of project
management is required for nearly every segment of a firm,
including sales, marketing, production, and publishing. Thus, there is
a need for project managers. Have you ever planned a gathering?
You oversaw a team of individuals on the project, and project
management is a talent that everyone should possess. Formally
speaking, projects arise in all business sectors and industries.
Finance and law
Building and Construction
Product manufacture
IT
Transport and infrastructure

# Chapter 2: Introduction to the PMP Exam

The Project Management Institute (PMI) is recognized worldwide and also offers a professional certification called Project Management Professional (PMP). Individuals who fulfill specific academic and experience requirements are granted PMP certification by the Project Management Institute (PMI). Professionals need to fulfill several prerequisites before they may submit an application for certification. To become a certified associate in project management, your application needs to be accepted by the project management institute, after which the candidate must pass a demanding and thorough exam. The well-acknowledged PMP certification is among the most advantageous features you may showcase on your CV. A certificate attesting to their qualifications is frequently necessary for applicants seeking positions as project manager, project executive, associate or assistant PM, or team manager.

## Maintaining Your Certification

After passing the test and earning their certification, professionals must maintain the requirements for continuing education if they wish to maintain their designation. To keep their certification, certificate holders need to complete sixty professional development units (PDUs) every three years. PDUs can be earned via a range of efforts, such as authoring articles for publications, public speaking, and full-time project management duties.

## What Is A PMP Certified Professional Expected To Know?

It is expected of applicants and exam takers that they have a thorough understanding of project management terminology, problems, and basic concepts. Since a number of project management techniques are applicable to a variety of industries, certified personnel are expected to be ready for a broad range of situations and results. Additionally, a plethora of first-hand project management experience is required of certificate holders.

## Minimum Requirements for Application

Anyone who wishes to apply for the exam to be certified has to fulfill one of two strict requirements. The minimum requirement for applicants is 7,500 hours of project management experience and 35 hrs of related courses. Alternatively, they can meet the requirements with a relevant 4-year degree, 4,500 hrs of project leadership experience, and 35 hrs of training in project management.

To get started with the procedure, aspirants have to generate a login for the Project Management Institute portal and provide the needed information. Both PMI members and non-members must pay an application fee; however, membership drastically lowers the price.

## Preparing For The Examination

Many people who apply for the PMP exam spend several weeks or months studying to be sure they have mastered the material contained in the course. The exam is divided into 5 parts: project initiation, project planning, project execution, project monitoring, and closing. The exam currently consists of 200 questions with multiple choices covering a variety of topics, such as conflict resolution and code of ethics.

## The Exam's Format And Style

We should now have a solid idea of what you should know and be able to do. Let's have a closer look at what the PMP test will entail.

We should now have a solid idea of what you should know and be able to do. Let's have a closer look at what the PMP test will entail.

## Exam Structure and Format for the PMP

You are allotted 230 minutes to complete the 180 PMP exam questions. Out of the 180 questions you have, 5 questions will not be counted towards the final marks; they are meant to determine whether or not will be assessed for future PMP examinations based on their results. In other words, 175 out of 180 questions will be used to determine your final grade. But, since the non-counting questions are dispersed randomly all through the examination, don't attempt to guess which of them they are. You must respond to each and every question;

How each area is weighted will determine how it is scored. Your proficiency with project management methods and concepts, such as:

Risk management
Planning and organizing,
Procurement management,
Monitoring and
Controlling

It's important to keep in mind that once you finish a part and continue, you cannot return to the previous questions. Thus, before continuing, be sure you have answered all the questions.
You may choose to take two ten-minute breaks. While some people would rather press through, I advise taking such breaks. The test is difficult and demanding. Resting is necessary, even if it's just for a little while. It will enable you to de-stress, find clarity, and sharpen your attention.

## Domains

In the past, the PMP tests were centered on 10 knowledge areas & 5 process groups. Although they remain an essential part of the test, the update has shifted its attention to 3 domains: people, processes, and the business environment. People: Your capacity for leadership as a project manager will be examined in this domain.

• Process: You will be required to demonstrate your technical project management skills in this domain.

• Business Environment: As the name suggests, this domain involves business settings. It will cover your business knowledge, compliance, and how to handle changes in organizational management.

Items You're Likely To See

You can come across a wide range of topics on the PMP exam. Let's discuss a few of them.

**10 areas of knowledge in project management**

Integration Management

Scope Management

Schedule Management

Cost Management

Quality Management

Resource Management

Communications Management

Risk Management

Procurement Management

Stakeholder Management

## Questions Related to Processes

In addition to the customary multiple-choice questions, PMI chose to provide a wider variety of question formats. These consist of fill-in-the-blank, drag-and-drop, and hot-spot questions.

### Multiple-Choice

You will be presented with a question or statement with 4 alternative answers to these questions. Out of the 4 only 1 is guaranteed to be right—the other 3 are distractions or incorrect answers. It's frequently difficult to tell apart the distractions. They frequently give the impression of being right, but they aren't. Remember that even though 2 or even 3 responses seem correct, you must select the best response for the particular topic or situation.

Answer certain questions right away if you know the answers, but you have to be 100 percent sure. Even though you're running out of time, take your time! For the time being, ignore any questions you are unclear about. But wait—don't go to the next section until you've answered questions in the present one.

Return to the questions you were unsure of after responding to those that you're certain about. Take out a few of the distractions first. You are already 50% likely to get the right answer if you rule out at least 2 of them.

## Multiple-Response

You will be required to select multiple responses from a list of potential answers to these questions. There will be more than 4 possible answers to some of those questions. Always select the best response, remember?

Questions are sometimes challenging. To select the right answers, you must take into account all of the information that has been provided. This is how they are offered. Most of these will be difficult for you to answer, but a couple might be clear-cut. Consider how each choice might complement the others you have selected. In the end, the solutions you select must complement one another to appropriately address the scenario.

## Here is an example of Multiple-Response Question

```
Due to a major delay in some scheduled tasks, the project manager had to
reprioritize several subsequent tasks to fix the problem. Unfortunately,
that didn't work either, and now the project manager must escalate the
problem.
Which documents must the project manager look at from the choices below to
escalate the issue? (Choose two answers)
A. Change management plan

B. Stakeholder engagement plan

C. Communications management plan

D. Risk management plan

E. Configuration management plan

Correct Answer: B and C
```

## Drag & Drop

You can rearrange a number of the items by simply dragging and dropping them into the proper position. To illustrate a project's life cycle, for example, you might be given different descriptions of its phases and required to drag and drop them into the appropriate order.

You'll need to properly or chronologically reorder the material. Additionally, meanings may be provided to you, which you must drag to the appropriate phrases, or vice versa.

## Hot Spot

A graph or diagram will be displayed to you, and you will be asked questions on it. In order to figure out the answer to the question, you must click on the displayed graph or diagram. You may occasionally need to click on many areas. You must click on the appropriate and pertinent location for the context or scenario that the question depicts; therefore, carefully consider the issue before answering it.

### Here is an example of Hot-Spot Question

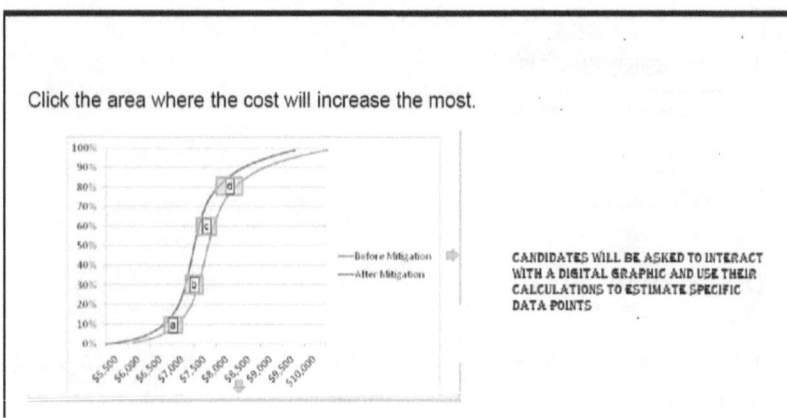

### Fill in the gaps.

This kind of question could appear all throughout the test. For example, in multiple-response or multiple-choice questions, you can be asked to select options that fill in portions of the given scenario.

Additionally, there can be tables or paragraphs with blank spaces that need to be filled in. In certain situations, there will be a box for you to fill in the details that are missing. This indicates that you are only done with the question when you have answered every blank.

**Here is an example of Fill in the Gaps Questions**

```
Question 33
Except for _____ all of the following are primary benefits of meeting
quality requirements:
A. Less redoing
B. Increased Productivity
C. Lowering expenses
D. Less change orders


Answer To Question 33 = D
Explanation: Data analysis approaches that can be utilized for this process
consist of, but don't just apply to cost-benefit analysis.
Every quality action has a cost-benefit analysis that weighs the expected
return against the expense of the quality step.
Less rework, more productivity, lower costs, higher stakeholder
satisfaction, and increased profitability are the main advantages of
satisfying quality standards.
The project manager will be able to assess the cost-effectiveness of the
planned quality activities with the use of a cost-benefit analysis.
The optimum option in terms of advantages offered can be found by
estimating the strengths and weaknesses of each alternative using a cost-
benefit analysis, a financial analysis method.
```

## How Is The PMP Exam Setup

There are 180 questions with multiple answers in the exam, which are based on the PMBOK standard and the Project Management Professional Code of Ethics. No reference books are permitted during the closed-book exam. Five out of the 180 exam questions are "sample" questions, meaning they do not determine the exam taker's score; instead, they are used to adjust the exam's level of precision and difficulty. These questions will appear at random across the exam. Just 175 questions out of the 180 questions are used to determine the exam taker's grade. The percentages in parentheses represent the number of questions within each domain.

## Who Is Eligible To Take The PMP Certification Exam?

The PMI offers the highly sought-after PMP certification, which is recognized globally. Being able to manage projects effectively is a valuable asset to any corporation, and it can be used in practically every type of business environment.

According to the Program Management Institute, obtaining the Project Management Professional certification entails applying knowledge, skills, and procedures to successfully complete projects. If a person fits the qualifications and wants to concentrate on project management or leadership, they should think about getting a certificate. There are thousands of PMI members worldwide, and the organization's PMI certification is acknowledged all around the world.

Professionals with a PMP certification not only have an advantage over others in the labor market, but they also earn more money. Additionally, the certification process helps candidates become experts in their field, which in turn helps them manage their teams effectively.

## Eligibility And Requirement To Sit For PMP Exam

You need to complete a particular number of PDUs (Professional Development Units) and have experience in a certain amount of professional project management before you can sit for the PMP certification exam.
You need to have had some experience beforehand.
When applying to get the certification, you have to make sure that all of your project management experience has occurred in the eight years prior.

**You have to meet at least one of the criteria listed below to get certified as a PMP:**

**Set 1:** A high school diploma or an associate's degree

A CAPM certification or 35 hrs of official project management training are required.
60 months of consecutive experience in project management over the previous eight years

**Set2:** A 4-year degree, or its world equivalent; 35 hours of official project management education; or a CAPM certification.
thirty-six months of uninterrupted project management expertise during the previous eight years.

## PMP Certification Exam Application Process

Candidates must fully understand every aspect of the exam before proceeding with the process, as they are not able to cancel their application and get a refund. Find below some of the steps and processes for the application:

**Step 1:** Go to the Project Management Institute website, register for a membership, and apply. It is advised to register for PMI membership in order to avoid incurring costs. However, there is a one-time cost of $139 to be paid. The one-time admission charge is $10, and newly admitted members must pay a membership fee of $129.

The advantages are reflected in the lower PMI application & examination retake fees.

The exam costs $555 for non-members on average, but only $405 for PMI members.

**Step 2:** Completing the PMP Certification Training Course will fulfill the prerequisites for the certification.
You can learn from the pros by enrolling for PMP certification training.

Your completion of the required 35 hours of instruction is aided by PMP Certification Training. The completion of this training program will award you a globally recognized certificate, which will help you get employment at a high-profile business. Furthermore, these courses come with exam papers to help with preparation.

**Step 3:** Submit Your Online Project Management Professional Application
Apply right now if you meet all the requirements for PMI certification. The institute typically gets back to you in 5 business days.

Once the application has been approved, you will receive an invitation at the scheduled time of the exam and pay the required money.

**Step 4:** Register for your Pearson VUE exam.
The approval of the application is good for a year. Within this period, you are allowed to retake the exam a maximum of three times. Exam centers and other options are available for candidates to select based on their financial situation.

Step 5: Get your certificate after passing the PMP certification exam. The examinee gets 230 minutes to complete the 180 questions available on the PMP exam to pass. Three types of questions are present:

Process (50%)
People (42%)
Business Environment (8%)

**PMP Membership And Fees:**
Once the application has been submitted, the PMI will email you a payment link for the exam. The examination costs USD $405 currently for members and USD $555 for non-members. Membership in PMI is optional, but there are many advantages to signing up for the membership.

The annual membership fee for PMI is $129. You will receive a complimentary digital copy of the PMBOK Guide upon joining; in addition, you will have free access to peer-reviewed articles, on-demand webinars, and business and project management books in e-Reads & Reference.

**PMI Audit Process:**
After you have successfully paid for the PMP examination fees, you can determine right away whether your application requires an audit or not. If your application is chosen for the Project Management Institute audit, you will have three months to produce documentation supporting each detail stated in it.
Proof of contact hours (printed certificate of contact hours)
Proof of education (photocopy of college/university degree)
A signed letter of recommendation for the contact person mentioned in the application's projects. Original, signed letters of

recommendation from each contact party are placed in separate envelopes with the contact person's signature appropriately covering the flap.

If the contact party is not available, any other person who is aware of the applicant's role can also carry out this particular procedure. Place all of these documents and proofs inside one sizable envelope and submit it via registered mail to the Project Management Institute. You are expected to receive a confirmation e-mail within one week.

**PMP Refund Policy for Examination Fees**
If you decide to drop your application to sit for the PMP exam, you must notify the Project Management Institute no less than 30 days prior to the exam eligibility deadline.

If you are yet to schedule or take the exam, your refund will be issued minus a $100 charge for processing. If you don't pass the audit, you get paid the same amount.

**Schedule of PMP Certification Exams**
Scheduling your test is the next step after completing the audit process along with additional requirements. To take the examination, you must select between a computer-based test (CBT) and a paper-based test (PBT) by logging into the Project Management Institute Certification system. The examination date you set must be within one year of the fee submission date.

The PMI examination is typically conducted via CBT, and PBT is only accessible in limited cases. If there are less than ten candidates for the PBT event, PMI has the right to cancel it. Candidates who wish to apply for a PBT examination venue must meet the requirements listed below:

must live 180.25 miles (300 km) away from the CBT location. The corporate sponsors prefer to carry out the test to staff members in the company's facilities.

## The PMP Certification Examination

There are a total of 200 tough questions in the PMP exam, comprising 175 multiple-choice questions that attract scores and 25 pretest questions that do not attract scores. The exam will take a total of 4 hours to complete. You need to correctly answer 137 questions to pass the test. You can arrange for another attempt if you are unable to pass the exam on your first try. You will be allowed to take the exam three times within a year.

After passing the exam, you will be given your PMP certificate between 6-8 weeks. Additionally, you can ask PMI to send a PMP lapel pin for free.

## Renewal of PMP Certification

Your 3-year PDU cycle starts after you pass the exam, and your PMP certification expires at the end of that period. To keep your PMP credential active, you must earn an extra Sixty PDUs per three-year PDU cycle. But, you can renew your PDUs without waiting for the three-year cycle to finish. During the certification year, you can earn 60 PDUs.

PMI has established two categories—Education and Giving Back to Profession—for obtaining additional PDUs. You will receive one PDU for every hour that you spend participating in professional development activities.

Education (PDUs earned have no maximum limit)

Attending workshops or seminars sponsored by PMI or PMI Registered Education Providers (R.E.P.) is one way to earn PDUs. PDUs can also be earned by attempting a PMI Publication Quiz, which requires studying an article and answering a minimum of 70% of the available questions correctly.

You can earn PDUs by passing an academic class sponsored by a university or by training organizations such as your workplace, corporates, or membership associations that are not registered with PMI. You can earn PDUs for non-formal learning activities like reading books, podcasts, and films, that are related to project risk, scheduling, project management, or program management. Returning the Favor to the Profession (not exceeding 45 PDUs in a three-year period)

You may also earn PDUs by expanding the body of knowledge in your area of expertise (by writing books, articles, webinars, speaking at project management courses, etc.).

PDUs can be obtained by offering non-employers non-compensated project management, project scheduling, or program management services.

Additionally, you can present letters or certificates from the company recognizing your contributions to project management. You must update the PDU Activity Reporting form, which is accessible on the PMI website, as soon as you begin participating in PDU-earning activities. You can submit a request for credential renewal after completing the three-year cycle with 60 PDUs earned. The renewal price is $60 for members and $150 for non-members. Your new certificate will arrive in the mail in six to eight weeks.

# Chapter 3: Introduction To The PMBOK Handbook

Businesses value PMBOK because it helps them prevent project failure by standardizing practices across departments and modifying practices to fit specific needs. The Project Management Body of Knowledge (PMBOK) is regarded by the international project management community as a comprehensive collection of rules about practices, protocols, and lexicon that should be followed by any organization and project manager.

Since experienced project managers always find new approaches or best practices, a body of knowledge has to be updated and shared frequently. This program is overseen by the nonprofit PMI, an association of project managers.
While PMBOK is not so much a methodology as it is an industry framework for best practices in project management, it is often linked to the "waterfall methodology," which aligns project stages in a sequential manner. One of the more modern approaches, agile, is also consistent with PMBOK.

Since PMBOK methods can be tweaked to match an array of project management conditions, the PMI does not endorse any one methodology. Rather, project managers select the protocols that make the most sense for their team, company, and projects.

**The PMBOK's Historical Background**
Project managers founded the PMI in 1969 because they felt it would be helpful for project managers to have a central location where they could communicate and discuss topics related to their line of work. In 1984, the PMP certification became the first to be given by the PMI. A PMBOK white paper was released in 1987, and the initial draft of the PMBOK Guide was released in 1994.

The Project Management Body of Knowledge (PMBOK Guide) is a reference book for project managers of all levels. The PMI originally released The Guide to the PMBOK in 1996. Its seventh edition, which comes in twelve languages, was published in 2021. But keep in mind that the seventh edition of the PMBOK Guide does not supersede the sixth edition. They can find project management terminology, basic standards, and guidelines in the PMBOK.

While managers seeking a process-based strategy will continue to use the sixth edition, those who prefer an approach based on principles will find the seventh edition to be very helpful. In contrast to earlier editions that were replaced by newer ones, the seventh edition expands upon the content included in the sixth edition.

Technology is utilized by most firms and is developing at an amazing rate. It follows that an update to the PMBOK Guide would be appropriate. Because of new technology, businesses are able to innovate and quickly shift the market.

**The PMBOK Guide has been updated in the following areas:**

• There is a section titled "Methods, Models, and Artifacts," along with a more extensive list of methods and resources.
• It includes all approaches to development, including hybrid, agile, adaptive, and traditional.
• The handbook emphasizes project outcomes in addition to deliverables.
• A comprehensive section on customizing strategy and procedures is included.
• The handbook offers more guidance on applying the PMBOK Guide in practical settings by utilizing PMI standards.

To put it briefly, the PMBOK Guide was revised to reflect developments in the international industry. As a result, project managers will find it useful and effective in setting, pursuing, and completing their goals. Let's discuss the important knowledge domains and process groups.

## Important Process Groups and Knowledge Areas

Let's take some time to examine the process groups and knowledge domains that are crucial to the success of the project. Learn a lot about them because they are the foundation of project management.

### The Knowledge Areas

In the following paragraphs, I'll go over the knowledge areas that can assist you in becoming a more skilled project manager in general and successfully supporting your project planning and execution efforts.

33

You should pay attention to these ten PMP knowledge areas since they will be crucial to your success on the test, but their significance extends beyond that.

### Project Stakeholder Management

Every project is created to fulfill the needs of a single person or a group of people. You will need to get familiar with them, pay attention to any problems or recommendations they may have, meet their needs, manage their expectations, and interact with them well. They are essential to the project's success because their dreams gave rise to it. Treat with caution!

### Project schedule management

Schedule management entails anticipating and arranging for potential problems. It will be your responsibility as a project manager to oversee each team member's timetable and deadline. That is made feasible by this field of expertise. Along with creating a project schedule, you will also provide your team members with instructions on what has to be done and when. This covers any adjustments that might be necessary to guarantee the project is finished on schedule.

### Project procurement management

This area of expertise is crucial if your project calls for the hiring of external vendors, contractors, or any other kind of resource. You must locate, choose, employ, oversee, and manage all external resources while keeping an eye on the project's budget.

## Project Risk Management

A larger project may entail greater hazards. Even if any of these risks materialize, planning with consideration will help you stay on the right path with your project. When you apply this knowledge areas will learn about risk prioritization, ,regulation planned responses, monitoring risk levels, and risk identification through quantitative and qualitative risk aassessment

## Project Communication Management

Never disregard the significance of clear communication. Following this expertise area entails maintaining contact with stakeholders, overseeing and managing all project-related correspondence, and making sure team members communicate clearly. But first, you have to figure out what kind of communication the project requires. You may sleep easier knowing that everything is proceeding as planned when you take this action.

## Project Resource Management

The degree to which you can effectively manage resources throughout the project will determine how successful it is. Project resources include things like team members, suppliers, materials, and tools. Accurate resource estimation, planning, development, acquisition, management, and control are all part of it.

## Project Quality Management

This knowledge area involves control, requirement, and end-to-end quality assurance from start to finish. In what other way could one establish and adhere to the standards of values within a project? Once more, you'll need to budget for any problems relating to the edibles' quality. It ought to be compatible with the project's spending plan and timeline.

## Project cost Management

Expectations will be required to complete your project, but they must be reasonable. To do this, you'll need to create a budget, monitor it, and stay on top of it. This will assist you in monitoring labor, supplies, equipment, and any other expenses that might be incurred.

## Project Scope Management

The project's scope serves as its framework and is designed to guarantee its success. Completing all the elements and meeting the deadline for the results depends on having a well-defined, verified, and managed scope. The project won't be hampered by irrelevant work if the scope is followed and appropriate expectations are set. Understanding this field will enable you and the other participants to stay focused on the project.

## Project Integration Management

Think of Project Integration Management as the big picture for your project. This vast section encompasses all the actions and duties required to finish the project that connect the start to the finish. You can also compare the project's objectives with the missions, visions, and ambitions of your business in this section. Does the project fit into these? Remember the stakeholders; you also need to take their objectives into account.

The PMP exam's focus has switched to three domains instead of the usual five following the most recent update: People, Process, and Business Environment. This does not, however, imply that important process groups and knowledge domains have disappeared. They merely exist as one of these three domains' subsets. The weighting of these categories is as follows: 42% are devoted to people, 8% are devoted to the business environment, and 50% are devoted to processes. This indicates a shift in emphasis toward processes.

Despite being primarily associated with the Process domain, the knowledge areas and process groups have representation in all three domains. Understanding the important knowledge domains and process groups can help you fully understand a project's natural flow as well as the pertinent concepts and procedures. It will help you determine which records, instruments, and strategies are appropriate for managing certain conflicts and situations.

## Consequences of the PMP Exam Changes

The major changes to the PMP test could provoke you to feel anxious or even confused. Understand that your knowledge and skills as a project manager are going to be tested, so keep that in mind.
Being a Project Management Professional (PMP) requires you to be flexible and responsive to ever-changing circumstances.

Your study schedule and strategies need to change to accommodate the PMP Exam Changes.

The growth of the project manager job in the corporate sector is the main cause behind the changes to the PMP exam. These PMP Exam Changes will ultimately be very helpful for settling into the business culture of any organization in the near future, as the curriculum will shift from being solely process-based to being multifaceted and covering all facets of PMP. The amount of time a candidate for the PMP can spend on the exam has likewise decreased. The previous structure required 240 mins to complete 175 multiple-choice questions. With a greater range of questions and 230 mins to score 175 of them, the PMP Exam features a new format that has expanded its scope.

The updated exam supports a wider variety of project management techniques and abilities. To improve one's chances of acing the examination on your very first attempt, even though the knowledge areas might not appear as noticeable as they once were, you still need to have a thorough understanding of them and the process groups.

Once more, incorporate the knowledge into your practice rather than just attempting to memorize it all. Recognize it and consider more about how the data might be applied in practical situations. That's why having real-world experience is extremely important. The PMBOK Guide contains information that you can use in your projects.
Gaining more knowledge about the structure and style of the PMP test will aid in your preparation.

The PMP Exam has a reputation for being one of the hardest tests in the world, so you must stop worrying about the updates and continue studying.

## Chapter 4: Why You Should Seek A Profession In Project Management

Like many other professions, project management requires the development of a broad variety of skills to succeed. Project managers should have great organizational skills, be competent problem solvers with above-average math skills, and be outstanding communicators. A career path in project management could be a good fit for people who enjoy handling different tasks.

**More reasons to seek a profession in project management include:**
1. There is a big difference that project managers can make. They directly affect the organization's bottom line in addition to staff morale. That's a really nice bonus to have on top of the excellent salary.
2. In today's market, project managers should expect competitive salaries. The typical base pay for an entry-level project manager is $54,132 annually, according to Indeed.
3. From 2021 to 2031, project management specialists' employment is projected to grow by 7%, or almost the same as the average growth rate for all occupations.
4. The market for project managers is highly competitive and in great demand. The Project Management Institute (PMI) predicts that there will be 22 million more project management jobs by 2027.
5. Acquiring new skills: As you study for the test, you'll probably pick up a lot of knowledge about project management. You can improve your project management abilities by dedicating several hours of your time to learning the principles of budgeting and conflict resolution.
6. Industry recognition: Possessing the PMP certification will demonstrate to potential employers or clients that you are knowledgeable about project management and possess the necessary training and experience for a professional.

To succeed as a project manager, what kinds of talents do you require?

## How to Evaluate Yourself as a Project Manager

If you're thinking about a career path in project management, it's imperative to evaluate yourself to see if you possess some of these abilities and characteristics required to be a successful project manager. Find out from the list below:

1. Skill to Handle Stress: It is expected that PMs should be able to handle the stress that comes with their job. The role of a PM is an important one and can be demanding and extremely accountable at times. Whatever happens, you should always remain composed.
2. Identifying and Managing Risks: How experienced are you at recognizing risks? Do you possess the skill to easily identify the possibility of a negative occurrence while on a project while simultaneously taking the risk assessment into account? You are PM material if you are skilled at it.
3. Flexibility & Open Mind: A project manager can face a range of challenges daily; while some of the challenges could be anticipated, some of the problems might be unexpected or planned for. Every day comes with new challenges and a never-ending series of new challenges for a PM. Therefore, in extremely uncertain situations, project managers need to be flexible and adaptable in order to approach new challenges with a positive attitude and a desire to use their creativity to solve difficulties.

4. Being a Meticulous Manager: If you are the kind of person who is detailed and organized when it comes to anything, then a project manager position can be well suited for you. PMs must pay close

attention to every detail to efficiently manage budgets, schedules, and resources.

5. Problem-solving mindset: project managers must have a positive outlook, problem-solving skills, and a solution-oriented mindset to successfully handle unexpected challenges or setbacks and overcome obstacles that may develop during a project. To put it simply, it's critical that PMs handle these circumstances with a positive attitude and a willingness to discover answers.

6. Capacity to Lead and Communicate: Project managers need to be experienced in both effective communication and motivating teams. If you enjoy taking responsibility and being in charge, a PM position can be the ideal fit for you.

**Skills you need to become a Project Manager**
Effective project management skills require a combination of hard skills such as risk and performance that can guarantee the smooth running of the project, along with soft skills such as motivation and communication. These skills are necessary because stakeholders as well as team members will look up to you for adequate direction.

1) Leadership Skills: There are a variety of leadership skills that are necessary for a project manager to possess, such as effective communication, problem-solving, decision-making, negotiation, interpersonal, team-building, and emotional intelligence. It is the duty of project managers to oversee the team's activities, pass information to stakeholders at all organizational levels, and manage client and management expectations. Therefore, it is expected of them to possess exceptional leadership skills, which include problem-solving, decision-making, team-building, communication, emotional intelligence, and interpersonal.

2) Managerial Skills: The greatest project management abilities that someone should have are the ability to control risk and to estimate, budget, and forecast in order to ensure that the project stays on schedule, is finished on time, and has no project overruns. Understand your industry from top to bottom, as well as the methods, techniques, and tools used in project management.

3) Business Skills: Project managers are expected to be very knowledgeable in business expertise to understand how project objectives and outcomes can be beneficial to the company, clients, and staff as a whole. Business skills help project managers make calculated decisions, prioritize tasks, and channel the project resources for proper use to guarantee good project outcomes.

4) Technical skills: These skills include an understanding of how to coordinate the action plan, finances, and scope of a project. Project managers should be able to handle technical skills such as planning and effectively monitoring projects while employing the right tools at the right moments.

**Top industries for project managers to seek employment in**
There are so many industries in the business setting that are looking for qualified project managers. Project management isn't limited to specific businesses but flows throughout a range of industries. The top industries for which project managers are needed are listed below:
Construction
Engineering
Manufacturing
Health Insurance

Architectural
Software/IT

What kinds of jobs can someone who has PMP certification undertake? Project Management Job Titles

**The following roles are common in the field of project management:**

1. Project Manager: A project manager is responsible for overseeing all the projects' budgets, project plans, project timetables, and product demos from beginning to end. The PM is responsible for working on the project using his initiative, either to work along with members of the management department or assign specific tasks. The person holding this responsibility is responsible for completing the project.

2. Director of Project Management: This person is tasked with the sole responsibility of guiding, instructing, and developing project management operations as well as the structure of the workflow. He has the responsibility of moderating the entire project by creating standards, protocols, and the needed tools to promote efficient project delivery. Project management experience ranging from five to six years, together with supplementary abilities, is usually required for a director.

3. Senior Project Manager: Just as the name implies, his position may include overseeing more than one project simultaneously and deciding which ones should be given attention. You will find a senior project manager, mostly a member of the bigger leadership staff.

4. VP of Operations, COO: This is also an important position charged with the responsibility of operations management, planning, and the coordination of all project-related operations. They also coordinate the entire project by establishing and implementing a set of rules and regulations for the smooth running of the project operation.  A vice president of operations also takes up the responsibility of supervising others and works with organizations to provide top-notch operational support.

5. Assistant Project Manager: As the name implies, he assists the project manager on matters that are related to bigger projects where he needs to take up unconcluded or unfinished tasks that the project manager has not yet completed.
He can also be assigned to work on a minor aspect of the project and also be asked to attend meetings on behalf of the project manager. The assistant regularly meets with the project manager to discuss any potential obstacles and to report on progress.


6. Project Scheduler: The project schedulers arrange work, set deadlines, and supervise the requirements of the project. They also provide support to the project managers regarding organizing, coordinating, and keeping an eye on the deadlines, as well as finding possible customers for the pitch deck.

7. The creation and dissemination of project reports fall within the purview of the seventh post, which is that of the project coordinator. The project coordinator is also a member of the management staff who assists with the project.

# Chapter 5: What You Need To Know Before You Attempt The Exam

**How difficult is it to pass the PMP Exam?**

The Project Management Professional (PMP) exam is set to test candidates in a wide range of skills and knowledge about project initiation, project planning, project execution, project supervising, and completion of projects. Although the exam can be a bit challenging for persons who are currently employed and trying to advance their careers by earning the PMP certification, The exam consists of situational interview questions and example answers that call for both a practical understanding of what project management entails and a solid understanding of the PMP framework.

According to many who have attempted the exam, they reported that the exam is difficult, claiming that barely sixty percent of people pass it on their first try. On the other hand, a person's past project management experience and exam preparation may have an impact on how challenging the test is. Some people in the labor force who have experience managing projects understand the exam to be quite easy to pass, while others may find it very difficult.

## 10 Easy Steps to Passing the PMP Exam:

1. Practice, practice, practice: Exams are a great tool to gauge your knowledge and pinpoint areas in which you need to strengthen your skills. Make an effort to complete as many practice tests as you can, and go over the answers to determine why you answered the questions correctly or incorrectly.

2. Acquire practical project management experience: Taking the PMP exam helps you know how effectively you can apply your understanding and techniques about project management to real-life situations. Having practical knowledge on how to manage projects is very important in the application of what you have learned and how to apply the knowledge you have gained from studying the PMBOK Guide in real-life situations.

3. Familiarize yourself with the PMP structure and guidelines: The PMBOK Guide, published by the Project Management Institute (PMI), serves as the foundation for the PMP test. It is imperative to read the PMBOK Guide cover to cover and comprehend the PMP framework and how it is used in practical situations.

4. Become familiar with the PMP exam format and contents: There are a total of 200 tough questions in the PMP exam, comprising 175 multiple-choice questions. It covers project management areas like planning, execution, monitoring and controlling, and closing.

5. Make use of study resources and enroll in a PMP Certification Boot Camp:

You can have access to a wide range of materials related to the PMP exam, which includes online courses, practice examinations, flashcards, and study guides. These materials can be very helpful in preparing you for the exam and ensuring that you completely understand the PMP exam content and framework.

6. Set up a study plan and ensure you follow it: Set up a study plan that can fit into your schedule and make you follow it strictly, reviewing and practicing on a regular basis. This timetable allows you to have adequate time for study.

7. Make Use of PMP Exam Simulators Online

Online practice examinations for the PMP are referred to as PMP simulators. They put the candidate to the test using questions that are identical in structure to those on the PMP exam. Their goal is to imitate the exam atmosphere as well, so you can get used to the pressure and time. They are an excellent means of determining your degree of readiness.

8. Check out the PMP Exam Prep Workshops Online

Online PMP test preparation classes are also offered. These virtual training programs are typically less costly than live seminars. Select the one that most closely matches your learning style. Before choosing one, do a lot of comparison shopping and read customer reviews.

9. Attend PMP Exam Prep Courses

If you require more one-on-one time or prefer a classroom environment, PMP exam prep seminars are a fantastic option. These are a terrific way to meet other aspiring project managers in your area, in addition to networking through a PMI® membership. One additional advantage of these seminars is that they typically satisfy the 35 contact hours needed to apply to take the PMP test.

10. Seek help from others: Attending a study group or interacting with other PMP applicants can offer you guidance and support, as well as help you keep focused and on track.

## Tips for Passing the PMP Exam

The PMP test demands a great deal of preparation to pass. Include the following strategies and tactics in your preparation, along with attending a PMP course, practicing past test questions whenever you can, and gaining a thorough understanding of the PMBOK ideas and vocabulary.

**Tips for the General PMP Exam**
1. Use an elimination method to find the correct answer.
2. Prioritize answering the questions using the PMBOK ideas, then take your experience into account. When they clash, the PMBOK prevails.
3. Effectively manage your time: Keep in mind that you have 80 seconds for every question. If an answer to a question slips through you, note it, go on, and, if you have time, return to it later.
4. Practice asking vague and wordy questions so you're ready for the ones you'll encounter.
5. Since guessing has no consequences, answer every question.
6. Take three to five full-length real-time practice exams to see how prepared you are for the test and to see when you consistently score higher than 80% on those assessments.
7. Get into the habit of ruling out the utterly improbable possibilities first.

8. You should commit all of the formulas to memory, particularly PERT and earned value.

### Tips for PMI Concepts

1. It is necessary to clearly identify roles and duties.
2. One of the best tools is the Work Breakdown Structure (WBS).
3. The project manager approaches the work with initiative, acting before a danger materializes and becomes an issue. This is a crucial idea that could have an impact on numerous exam questions. Problems are not escalated to higher management or the client before the project manager has thoroughly examined them and determined all available solutions. If someone asks you what a project manager should do in a particular circumstance, you should rephrase the question to ask what the project manager will do first given the circumstances and their proactive style.
4. Project managers possess a wide range of hard and soft talents.
5. PMI disapproves of the addition of new functionality without advantages or fancy packaging.
6. Consider that previous databases and lessons learned are accessible. This might not hold true in practical circumstances.

### Question-based Suggestions

1. The right response might not be grammatically accurate.
2. Keep an eye out for options that represent unique situations. Words like often, sometimes, may, generally, and probably characterize these choices, which are usually accurate.
3. Watch out for response selections that indicate generalizations; these are frequently the wrong ones and can be identified by terms like always, never, must, or fully.

4. Rather than responding to the questions from your own, experience-based perspective, you must respond from a PMI perspective. Keep in mind that PMI may not accurately reflect the ideal environment you have experienced as a project manager.
5. There is just one right response to each question. You must choose the best response possible. Selecting options that convey true claims but lack context should be avoided. Before choosing an option, make sure to read through them all.
6. Some questions have more information in them. This information is unrelated to the right response and is therefore irrelevant. Be wary of such inquiries, and keep in mind that you don't have to use every piece of information offered to address the inquiry.

# Chapter 6: Project Management Terms To Be Familiar With

Professionals in every field have their own set of terminology that they use to express demands and expectations related to business. Many different industries' project managers utilize a large lexicon that is unique to their industry. It is beneficial for professionals to keep up with new project management words as the discipline incorporates new concepts and approaches.

I will explain a few management terms that will improve your knowledge of project management and enable you to interact with others more effectively in the workplace.

**What terminologies are used in project management?**
Managers can use management words, which are phrases unique to their sector or firm, to give meaning, establish expectations, or establish a shared language with their teams. These terms usually specify the criteria of the organization or represent a work procedure, industry-specific skill, tool, or expectation. Project management, people management, corporate management, and other leadership domains frequently use these phrases. Management terms to help strengthen your knowledge and understanding of the field:

1. Work-in-progress limit
The maximum number of jobs that can be ongoing at once is decreased by the work-in-progress limit. The cap keeps teams from building up an unfinished backlog of work throughout a project. This can improve the efficiency of projects and the distribution of resources by reserving resources for ongoing tasks exclusively.

2. Work-in-progress (WIP)
A task or set of tasks that a team is working on at the moment is called a work-in-progress. One can also designate a work in progress

that is being examined as a WIP. WIPs give managers a better idea of what the finished product might look like and allow them to modify or recommend changes before they are finished.

3. Work breakdown structure (WBS)
Bigger jobs are broken down into smaller ones using a work breakdown structure. Chunking project facilitates managers' ability to communicate project responsibilities and schedule time to guarantee job completion. Employee morale can be preserved by giving them smaller tasks, which may also prevent burnout or dissatisfaction with large project requirements.

4. Workstream
The group of related tasks needed to finish a project is called a workstream. Some projects require the completion of a prior project in order to be worked on. Managers can use this to more precisely allocate resources and help them prioritize activities.
46. Waterfall model
The waterfall model is based on a project's stages being developed in order from start to finish. There is minimal job overlap or modification in the waterfall process throughout the project's life cycle, in contrast to the Agile methodology. Professionals in manufacturing and development frequently use this technique.

5. Stand-up meeting
A daily scrum, sometimes referred to as a stand-up meeting, is a project's life cycle report that updates stakeholders on the project's status. To track progress and make sure the team allots enough time to finish each task within a project, the team members must provide regular updates during the meeting. Attending daily meetings can also boost output and morale.

6. Stakeholders

Stakeholders are those, external or internal, who have shown interest in seeing a project through to completion. Customers, staff members, company owners, and other people with a "stake" in the project's success might all be considered stakeholders. Stakeholders usually anticipate a return on their time or resource commitment.

7. Change control

Change control entails monitoring and carrying out requests throughout the project process. This reduces the possibility of scope creep or unregulated modifications throughout the project and gives managers the ability to approve or reject changes across the project scope. By doing this, you can make sure that the project stays on course and within the initial budget that the client or management specified.

8. Sprint

Throughout the project, a sprint is a chunk of time that gives project teams the opportunity to focus on a particular body of work. Planning, executing, and reviewing coordinated tasks that support the introduction of a product or service are all included in a sprint. Sprints strive to finish projects rapidly but efficiently to get the most resources and revenue.

9. Slack

The entire amount of extra time allotted to fixing mistakes or setbacks in the project scope is known as slack. Once project managers have determined how much slack is available during a project's life cycle, they can modify workloads as well as resources for the duration of the project. Less slack could indicate just a slight margin for error that could have a major impact on the business or project, while more slack might indicate more room for error but less time to finish the job.

## 10. Scrum
Scrum is an Agile approach that emphasizes taking small, manageable actions to finish a project. Scrums track a project's progress using sprints, or brief intervals. To accomplish a project's objectives, team members use sprints to provide parcels of progress. The approach promotes collaboration across departments and teams and might assist teams in becoming more effective.

## 11. Scope
The entire number of tasks and resources needed to finish a project is its scope. The scope is updated as the client or team adds additional demands or resources to the project life cycle. A project's scope also determines its size, which in turn determines the staffing and technical requirements.

## 39. Risk mitigation
Taking steps to reduce the likelihood of risks in a project team's daily operations is known as risk mitigation. Strategies for risk mitigation will forecast potential hazards and create plans to keep the project life cycle consistent. This is a dynamic process that is frequently managed by the stakeholders or project managers.

## 12. Risk management
The goal of risk management is to identify risks that could affect a project's scope and reduce those risks' effects across the project's life cycle. Risk management responsibilities include making sure regular operations and project objectives continue without incident. It can also guarantee that a business doesn't take unneeded or hazardous risks to preserve the integrity or quality of a project.

## 13. Resource management

Planning, scheduling, and resource management are all part of resource management, which guarantees that projects are completed on schedule. It is normal practice to measure time, performance, and cost concerning an organization's objectives.

## 14. Resource leveling

Resource leveling modifies the project scope to guarantee that resources are not used more than their intended use. The goal of a human resources leveling initiative is to keep team members from putting in excessive amounts of overtime. This might assist a business in sticking to its spending plan and reducing or eliminating needless expenses and hazards.

## 15. Resource calendar

When a team member or other resource is available to help with project-related tasks, it is indicated on a resource calendar. Resource calendars allow the team to plan ahead and account for the chance that some resources won't be available when needed. A resource calendar, for instance, can be used by a project manager to schedule employee vacation needs.

## 16. Resource breakdown structure

Every resource needed to finish a project is listed in the resource breakdown structure. Resources are arranged in a hierarchical framework according to their type and category. This could enhance the project's financial planning and structure.

## 17. Resource allocation

Appropriate distribution of resources, income, and labor is necessary to guarantee a project's completion. To meet the needs of the project scope, resource allocation focuses on optimizing a resource's consumption. Resource allocation is frequently handled by project managers.

## 32. Quality management plan

Plans for quality management set forth the standards, regulations, and directives necessary to comply with the organization's quality policy. The strategy makes sure that before a product or service is made available to stakeholders, the organization's and its quality requirements come first. In order to ensure that customers are receiving the best possible product or service, businesses occasionally discuss their plans with their clients.

## 18. Quality assurance

The purpose of quality assurance is to ascertain whether a good or service satisfies requirements. Audits are required to make sure a project meets all of the quality standards specified in the project scope. To retain its professional reputation, the company must make sure that it only offers the best goods or services, which is another benefit of quality assurance.

## 19. Project Timeline

This includes all of the time allocated to executing a project. To guarantee that a project stays within the corporate budget, the timetable takes into consideration every stage of the project's life cycle. Timelines provide the team with a rigid time frame, which might inspire them to produce their best work by the deadline.

## 20. Project portfolio management (PPM)

PPM is the process of managing project portfolios to analyze both big and small objectives that a business may have. PPM enables company executives and other team players to look at the larger picture underlying the scope of a project and link its successful completion to the organization's goals.

## 21. Project manager

Project managers supervise all facets of a project's execution, including labor, materials, and costs incurred during the project's life cycle. The ability to plan, monitor, and modify phases to guarantee smooth project progress is critical to the manager's success. In addition to supporting their teams, managers may also interact with clients regularly.

## 22. Project management

Project management uses labor, cash, and resources to satisfy stakeholder demands and expectations by completing projects. A thorough grasp of what is required and expected of a project is essential to project management. Effective project management frequently necessitates a good manager as well as the appropriate project software.

## 23. Project budget

The funds allotted to the realization of a project and its phases constitute the project budget. The budget can be arranged by project teams into an extensive document that details the resources and costs associated with each activity in the project. By doing this, the team will be better able to estimate the resources needed for each project and bill future clients for the same services.

## 24. Monitoring

A project's ability to be finished on schedule and within budget is determined by monitoring. Reports, graphical dashboards, and additional documentation are tools that project teams can use to monitor the project plan. Providing regular information to the client is another benefit of monitoring.

## 25. Lean project management

Lean project management emphasizes production and effectiveness from the customer's point of view by achieving more with less. The approach assists project managers in determining which procedures will optimize output while minimizing resource waste. Cutting waste can frequently boost a business's profits and the team's morale considerably.

## 26. Kickoff meeting

The first meeting between a client and the project team is known as the kickoff meeting. It lays forth the goals of a project and the timeline for its accomplishment. Before beginning, the meeting enables both parties to go over the project scope.

## 27. Kanban

Kanban is a schedule system for lean and just-in-time production. The interface encourages team members to change cards to show their progress in the project scope, resembling a virtual billboard. Kanban is widely used in manufacturing, development, and certain construction-related fields.

## 28. Just-in-time production

This is described as a production inventory system that ensures that only the resources needed to finish a project are used in this process called just-in-time production. Its goal is to reduce costs and boost efficiency. The goal of this approach is to increase project efficiency. The company can cut down on mistakes and errors by minimizing the number of personnel and assets involved.

## 29. Issue tracking

Issue tracking is designed to find errors and bugs that have an adverse effect on the final product or service. With the use of issue-tracking methods, project teams can record emerging problems and designate the right team to handle them. This method differs from an issue log, which is a physical record of past issues, and tracking, which is the process of actively monitoring every current issue.

## 30. Issue Log
Issue logs involve the documentation of all errors and bugs that occur during the project and in the final product or service. This will include the issue's details, the person or people tasked with resolving it, and all other relevant data. This generates historical records regarding every problem for future research.

## 31. Issue management
Issue management is designed to identify and record issues as they arise during a project. Effective issue management finds solutions for issues before they get bigger. Issue management is one example of a preventative technique that frequently helps reduce excessive costs or other issues.

## 32. Hybrid approach
The hybrid methodology combines the best aspects of both waterfall and agile approaches to increase a project team's productivity. In industries where timely, high-quality deliverables have an impact on costs or profitability, hybrid techniques are common. For instance, hybrid approaches are frequently used in software or online development.

## 33. Gantt chart
Project managers can allocate timetables, personnel, and material resources appropriately by using a Gantt chart, which is a horizontal bar chart that shows the overview of a project. Numerous sectors use Gantt charts, which are essential for many contemporary project management software programs. Gantt charts can be made by managers utilizing online templates or software.
Image of a sample grant chart

## 34. A feasibility study

Feasibility studies examine several project components to ascertain whether it is feasible to finish a suggested project. They do this by examining resources, costs, schedules, and other elements to give an in-depth understanding of the project's viability. The team may gain a better understanding of what it could take to provide the greatest deliverable as a result. It also assists a client in determining whether the team is appropriate for the request or project.

## 35. Estimation

Estimates serve as indicators to assist teams in analyzing the factors that go into finishing a project. Indicators such as personnel, money, and time are frequently used to evaluate how much work a team can finish with the fewest resources. When pitching a potential client, estimates can be helpful in giving them a rough estimate of how much your services will cost as well as how you can best serve their needs.

## 36. Dependencies

Dependencies involve the relationships that exist between products or tasks that affect how successfully a project is completed. Multiple dependencies are common in projects; these dependencies can include customer expectations, financial constraints, and the degree of departmental and team collaboration. New dependencies can be established by managers as needed for specific projects.

## 37. Deliverables

Deliverables are objective or tangible items that serve as benchmarks at the end of a project. Deliverables can take many different forms, including final items, documentation, and reports. These are the last components that a client sees and uses to evaluate the team's performance.

## 38. Dashboard

A dashboard shows statistics, project data, and any other resources that are required to finish a project. The dashboard has changed with the times, giving project teams access to real-time information whenever they need it. These tools are frequently found on platforms for project or personnel management.

## 39. Critical path method

Project managers often use the critical path technique, which is an algorithm that helps teams plan out their work. The phrase "critical path" refers to a project's schedule that takes the shortest route to completion. Finding the critical path might be useful in estimating the overall amount of time needed to finish a project.

## 40. Cost overrun

An unforeseen expense that develops during a project's life cycle is called a cost overrun. Teams may be inconvenienced by cost overruns and may even be required to reallocate resources to solve issues that fall within the project's scope. Managers frequently set stringent budgets for projects and constantly monitor expenditures to avoid this.

## 41. Contingent

When a problem arises that the team is unable to handle normally, contingencies are put in place as safety measures. Contingencies solve a wide range of issues and keep the project from stalling. They also assist in the planning of the management or business when costs, desired outcomes, or team performance change.

## 42. Collaboration

Collaboration entails team members taking an active role in

project activities. Successful project cooperation necessitates adequate planning, delegation, and communication among all team members during the project's duration. Since a lot of projects call for great teamwork, managers frequently put a lot of effort into encouraging positive relationships among team members to aid in the development of this vital talent.

## 43. Business plan

A business plan lays out the objectives of a project as well as the procedures required to reach them. The plan outlines the rationale behind initiating a project and contains crucial details like the activities, resources, and return on investment (ROI) needed to guarantee the project's success. A startup company's ability to draw in investors and its earliest supporters may depend on its business plan.

## 44. Bottleneck

When issues with the workflow of a project impede its advancement, it results in a bottleneck. When a project's workflow exceeds the resources allocated to it, bottlenecks can develop. Managers usually act fast to identify, resolve, and prevent bottlenecks because they can result in lost time and money.

## 45. Baseline

For every project, a baseline serves as a clear starting point. Baselines track the performance of a project for every team member and are updated in response to major changes made by clients, team members, or managers. Baselines also assist in setting expectations for everyone participating in the project.

## 46. Backlog

Every task needed to finish a project is included in the backlog. Over the course of a project, backlogs are accessible to all participants and assist industries in keeping track of all the elements necessary for its success. This can aid managers in comprehending the requirements and status of a project more precisely.

47. Agile project management
Agile project management is a common approach that encourages rapid project turnarounds and flexible work cultures. The agile technique breaks down projects into manageable chunks, known as sprints, and prioritizes activities. In the fields of software and online development, this phrase is frequently used.

# Chapter 7: Time To Practice

## Question 1
A project manager ensures that the workplace environment of his team is healthy by offering secure employment, competitive pay, and a focus on work appreciation. Which of the following describes a hygiene component, as described by Herzberg? (Choose three.)
A. Appreciation
B. Safe working conditions
C. Salary
D. Job security

## Question 2
Here is the definition of the precedence diagramming technique (PDM):
A. When project activity durations are unknown, this scheduling method is more accurate than the critical route technique.
B. An illustration of the arrow diagramming technique (ADM) that shows the dependencies and durations of project activities in a time-phased graphic format.
C. A method for scheduling project activities that takes a probabilistic approach.
D. An approach wherein tasks are graphically connected by one or more logical connections and portrayed as nodes to show the order in which they should be completed.

## Question 3

A team member has demonstrated great technical proficiency and the capacity to do all of their assignments on schedule. The team member was consequently promoted to the position of project manager by the CEO of the company. The actions of the CEO exemplify the:

A. Halo Effect
B. McGregor's Theory of X and Y
C. Expectancy Theory
D. Herzberg Theory

## Question 4

All of the following procedures are part of project cost management, with the exception of:

A. Control costs
B. Determine budget
C. Level resources
D. Plan cost management

## Question 5

A project manager gave a presentation on a football stadium construction project they thought would be extremely beneficial to the community. Even though the mayor agreed to see the project through to completion, the project manager faced strong opposition from a number of parties right from the start. What steps should the project manager take to address this issue?

A. Instead of approaching these stakeholders at the outset of the project, establish a "faits accomplis" to exert pressure on them to accept it because there are no other options.
B. Call a meeting with the relevant stakeholders to assure their involvement, go over the project in detail, go over and establish

ground rules, and identify any personal or organizational difficulties that may come up later.

C. Make an organizational diagram that places each stakeholder in the proper project role and allows for or restricts specific channels of communication.

D. Make a Responsibility Assignment Matrix (RAM) to list all the stakeholders who need to be contacted or informed about what components of the project they are responsible for.

## Question 6

What is the Component of the quality management plan, which explains how the organization's quality policies will be executed?

A. Governance management plan
B. Project scope
C. Program management plan
D. Project management plan

## Question 7

An organization that makes use of extrinsic motivators to boost team spirit and efficiency employs a project manager. In order to ensure that the team follows the corporate policy, what incentives could the project manager provide? (Select three.)

A. Allow team members to work on tasks they enjoy
B. Praise team members for their hard work
C. Offer a $10,000 bonus for the most performant team members
D. Create an "Employee of the Month" award

## Question 8

In order to ensure that projects and products meet quality standards, project quality management includes techniques for incorporating the organization quality policy:
A. Meet the performance expectations of the project team
B. Hold onto control over products, services, and results
C. Enhance process capabilities
D. Meet stakeholders' objectives


## Question 9

Within four months of project execution, the project manager saw that while some team members were performing poorly, others were still performing well. How can the project manager help the team get back on track?
A. Determine the reasons behind poor performance, get systematic feedback, and put appropriate fixes in place in light of the conclusions.
B. Let team members make improvements to their performance without getting involved.
C. Include a competitive compensation structure that provides a bonus for high performers to encourage underperforming team members.
D. Talk honestly about some team members' poor performance with the entire group to find a solution as a group.

## Question 10
Nearing the end of the project, a significant stakeholder approached the project manager asking if they were anxious about getting the project deliverables approved. The manager answered that they were sure the client would be happy with the outcome. What can guarantee the client's pleasure with the project?
A. Delivering value and conforming to project requirements
B. The efficiency of the warranty service
C. How good the project manager's relationship is with the project's end-users and stakeholders
D. The project's low running costs


## Question 11
Resource acquisition is the process of confirming that resources are available and putting together the team needed to complete project tasks. With the exception of the previously mentioned, the following enterprise environmental elements are usually susceptible to affecting this process:
A. Policies related to personnel administration, including those that impact outsourcing
B. competence level, past experience, and cost rate
C. Political Philosophy
D. The organizational structure

## Question 12
 The following factors all impact how long the activity takes, with the exception of:
A. applying precedence diagramming method (PDM) instead of the critical path method (CPM) for task scheduling
B. The resources assigned to the activity are available
C. The resources allotted to the activity
D. anticipated resource needs for the activity

## Question 13
A project manager has been pushing their team to be self-organizing since using the agile approach by giving them autonomy over how to carry out their allocated tasks. What makes a self-organizing team unique?
A. It gives the team members a better visibility of the product
B. It gives the team chance to deliver a functional product without external dependencies
C. It gives more responsibility to the Agile team
D. It gives more responsibility to the project manager

## Question 14
A project manager with PMP certification has over 20 years of experience as a designer in the automotive industry in addition to extensive knowledge of project management. Her most recent task was overseeing a team of designers as they created a fresh look for a futuristic automotive model. Given that the team has faith in her judgment, what authority does the project manager have?
A. Persuasive
B. Formal
C. Expert
D. Referent

## Question 15
Choosing the right kind of communication technology can be influenced by all of the following factors:
A. Sensitivity and confidentiality of the information
B. Executive requirements
C. Availability of technology
D. Urgency of the need for information

## Question 16
What is the main goal of configuration management?
A. identifying, recording, and managing changes to the project and product baselines; in other words, change control is concentrated on the details of the deliverables and procedures.
B. Testing new systems
C. The outline of both deliverables and processes, whereas change control focuses on identifying, recording, and accepting or rejecting changes to project papers, deliverables, or baselines.
D. Finding and fixing issues that crop up in project implementation's functional areas

## Question 17
Understanding, specifying, assessing, and managing needs are essential for achieving:
A. Functional requirements
B. Upper management
C. The scope statement
D. Customer expectations

## Question 18
A project manager oversees a team of remote workers that are spread out across several geographic locations. The project manager learns that certain participants misunderstood, overlooked, or forgot what was covered in the last meeting during a virtual biweekly retrospective. How can this be resolved by the project manager? (Select two)
A. Instead of holding meetings every two weeks, consider holding them once a week to ensure that team members remember what was discussed.
B. Make sure you record meetings and distribute the tapes to all participants.
C. Establish a new meeting convention wherein participants

must raise their hands to indicate what they don't understand.
D. Request that every team member attempt to speak English using an American accent.

## Question 19
A few of the inputs into the Plan Communications management process include the following:
A. Project management plan, enterprise, project documentation, organizational process assets and environmental variables
B. Organizational structure, stakeholder analysis, and communication obstacles in project management
C. Stakeholder requirements, budget, project scope statement, and timeline
D. Organizational process assets, enterprise environmental factors, project documentation, and a project management plan.

## Question 20
A project manager is in charge of an educational initiative. After performing a power analysis of the 4 project stakeholders, it was found that Monica and Markus have high power, whereas Ravi and Sergio have low power. To better understand, the project manager created the stakeholder involvement assessment matrix that is shown below.

| Stakeholder | Unaware | Resistant | Neutral | Supportive | Lea |
|-------------|---------|-----------|---------|------------|-----|
| Monica      |         |           | X       |            |     |
| Markus      | X       |           |         |            |     |
| Ravi        |         |           |         | X          |     |
| Sergio      |         | X         |         |            |     |

Based on this analysis, which stakeholder's engagement should be prioritized?
A. Sergio
B. Ravi
C. Markus
D. Monica

## Question 21
Culture consists of all of the following, with the exception of:
A. Values
B. Norms
C. Intelligence
D. Beliefs

## Question 22
After the project has been running for a month, the project manager discovers that the sponsor often arrives late for their weekly meetings. The project manager, however, decides not to confront the sponsor's actions. Rather, they record their habitual tardiness in the minutes of the meetings. Which method of resolving conflicts is the project manager employing?
A. Problem-solving
B. Smoothing
C. Information recording
D. Withdrawal

## Question 23
Creating a document that connects product needs from source to deliverables to guarantee that each requirement delivers business value as well as manages product scope changes. It's known as:

A. Requirements traceability matrix system
B. New product development matrix
C. Business case
D. Configuration management

## Question 24
What are the outcomes of the Define Scope process?
A. Scope and schedule delay control plan

B. Project scope statement
C. Resource breakdown structure (RBS)
D. Work breakdown structure (WBS)

## Question 25
With regard to the work breakdown structure (WBS), which of these sentences is true?
A. The WBS is a hierarchical breakdown of the overall scope of work to be completed by the project team in order to complete the project objectives and provide the requisite deliverables.
B. The WBS is a comprehensive list of chart that contains project activities.
C. The WBS is also referred to as the organizational breakdown structure OBS
D. The work breakdown structure (WBS) is the list of materials required to fulfill the project's goals and deliver the necessary deliverables.

## Question 26
A Project manager discovered shortly after they started a new project that one of their team members from mean earlier project was not producing as much as she used to. She agreed to a one-on-one meeting with the project manager and vented about not getting the performance bonus she had hoped for from her previous task. Which hypothesis is being used here?
A. Expectancy Theory
B. Anticipation Theory
C. Theory Y
D. Theory X

## Question 27
One method of schedule compression that adds resources to reduce schedule time while incurring the least additional expense known as:
A. Fast tracking
B. Precedence Diagramming Method (PDM)
C. Program evaluation and review technique (PFRT)
D. Crashing

## Question 28
Companies often attempt to finish projects with limited funds and unclear timelines. Adopting an agile approach can help handle such complexity. However, this plan will not achieve its goals if there is ineffective communication. What form of communication is appropriate for a project manager in this scenario?
A. Daily
B. Frequently
C. Formally
D. Informally

## Question 29

A senior project manager is employed at a medical device company that has experienced major organizational changes recently. A crucial team member informs the project manager that she is worried about a new hire because she doesn't think they have the technical skills necessary to complete the work they were given. What should the project manager do regarding this new team member, given their confidence in the member's judgment?

A. Release the new team member.

B. Nothing should be done since the concerned team member has already been assigned.

C. Provide the new member with training and mentoring.

D. Keep the new team member, but reassign their tasks to someone else.

## Question 30

Regarding cost estimations, every statement below is accurate, with the exception of _____.

A. A cost estimate is a quantitative assessment of the expected costs for the resources required to complete the task.

B. Cost projections should not incorporate information from the risk register since risks might be opportunities or threats, and their effects usually cancel out.

C. The costs of all resources that will be charged to the project are estimated.

D. Cost estimates are frequently given in monetary units (such as dollars, euros, yen, etc.); however, in some circumstances, other units of measurement—like staff hours or staff days—are employed to make comparisons easier by mitigating the effects of exchange rate fluctuations.

## Question 31

As a project manager, you are employed by Smart Heart Co. A company called Smart Heart makes medical supplies. You keep an eye out for any changes in the business environment that might have an impact on your project. PESTEL analysis is what you're utilizing to scan the surroundings. Which of the following is not a category that falls under PESTEL?

A. There are rumors that one of the project team members who recently quit will be working for Smart Heart's competitor.

B. A new technical product from Vital Pro, a rival of Smart Heart, has the potential to revolutionize the market.

C. The usage of Smart Heart's goods is prohibited in one of the countries due to political tensions.

D. As you operate in the US market, a new rule pertaining to healthcare products was introduced by the FDA.

## Question 32

A project manager oversees a branding initiative for a chain of fast food restaurants. A disagreement arose between two team members regarding a design assignment during the project. The project manager arranges a meeting with the two team members. They all agreed that outsourcing this task would be the best course of action after talking about it. What method of resolving conflicts did the project manager employ?

A. Forcing
B. Collaborating
c. Compromise
D. Smoothing

## Question 33

The following are the main advantages of achieving quality norms, with the exception of _____:
A. Less redoing
B. Increased Productivity
C. Lowering expenses
D. Less change orders

## Question 34

A national bank project manager chooses to schedule stakeholder interaction using the power/interest grid. What is the best way for him to handle a stakeholder who is interested but has little authority?
A. Monitor
B. Manage closely
C. Keep informed
D. Keep satisfied

## Question 35

What is meant by portfolio management?
A. Using resource leveling heuristics to achieve all of the strategic goals of the company
B. the central administration of one or more portfolios in order to accomplish strategic goals
C. Controlling the degrees of financial authority to help with project decision making
D. Organizing multiple components of the project file.

## Question 36

A groundbreaking medical research project is being led by a project manager. In a meeting time with the sponsor, the PM outlines his approach to managing the work, emphasizing his desire to promote self-awareness, coaching, and listening. The project manager continues, saying that one of his main goals is to support the team's growth. What style of management is the project manager planning to use?

A. Transformational leadership
B. Transactional leadership
C. Authentic leadership
D. Servant leadership

## Question 37

The following actions are involved in schedule compression using the "fast-tracking" method:

A. placing "dedicated teams" in charge of important path tasks in order to finish projects on time.

B. introducing a "necessary overtime plan" to finish the job as soon as possible, if not sooner

C. executing tasks or stages that are normally completed in order in parallel for at least some of the time, which could lead to more risk and rework

D. Industrial engineering techniques are applied to boost production and finish the project earlier than expected.

## Question 38

A project manager steps in to take over for a previous manager who left the company without warning. They discovered after the first week of work that the atmosphere at work was unproductive and that team members did not trust or support one another's ideas. In line with Tuckman's paradigm, what

stage of development is this team in?
A. Adjourning
B. Norming
c. Forming
D Storming

## Question 39
The various organizational behaviors that contribute to a project's complexity comprise the following aspects, except for:
A. System behavior
B. Human behavior
C. Ambiguity
D. Process behavior

## Question 40
Parametric estimating entails:
A. Defining project life cycle cost and duration parameters
B. Creating independent cost estimates for each work package and combining them to determine the final project cost
C. utilizing a statistical relationship between relevant historical data and other variables to create a cost estimate for project work
D. Calculating the current project's cost based on the actual cost of a previous, comparable project

## Question 41
Tom is employed by StateEx, a nationwide logistics organization, as a project manager. Tom is in charge of a project that will streamline delivery routes for business cars in an effort to save gasoline. One of the project team members, Victoria, sent you an email stating that she was unclear about her responsibilities. What ought to you do after that?

A. Bring up this matter at the upcoming team meeting and request that the team make Victoria's tasks more clear.

B. Set up a private meeting with Victoria to try to figure out what she doesn't comprehend.
C. Put a call across to Victoria's functional manager and double-check that she is qualified to work on the project.
D. Respond via email, advising her to re-read the project scope paper.


## Question 42
Define a program?
A. sequence of tasks that make up a major project
B. large-scale projects involving a lot of resources and money
C. A collection of connected projects, subsidiary programs, and program activities that are managed in a coordinated fashion.
D. a collection of connected projects that last a year or lesser

## Question 43
Electronic communications management, scheduling, and project management software web interfaces are examples of:
A. Project records databases
B. Internal management systems (IMS)
C. Internal communications systems (ICS)
D. Project management information systems (PMIS)

## Question 44

A project manager works with a company that makes kitchen appliances. The project manager was informed to begin getting ready for this change by their superiors, who made the decision to implement lean methods. What kind of authority are the project manager's superiors using?
A. Legitimate
B. Referent
c. Expert
D. Situational

## Question 45

The following are examples of project management office structures found in organizations, WITH THE EXCEPTION of:
A. Directive PMOs that take charge of projects by overseeing them directly
B. Harmonizing PMOs work to prevent friction and enhance harmony within project teams.
C. Controlling PMOs that use different methods to demand compliance and offer help
D. supportive PMOs that help with consultation and supply templates, best practices, training, information access, and lessons gained from previous projects to projects.

## Question 46

A project manager works to create an atmosphere at work that values exchanging ideas, creativity, and innovation. They schedule frequent team meetings to go over risks and concerns related to the project. In what capacity is the project manager seeking a leadership position?
A. Laissez-faire
B. Transformational

C. Interactional
D. Transactional

## Question 47
You oversee a project worth $10 million. For the purpose of "re-baselining" the project, which of the following justifies its approval?

A. A new $250,000 CAD system has been implemented by the performing organization's technology department.
B. Due to the design department's lower than anticipated productivity, 1,000 more hours have been worked than originally planned, and a two-week delay in the completion date is predicted.
C. The contractor's company has committed to investing $1 million over the course of the following year on a quality assurance program.
D. The project's scope has been expanded with the client's approval, resulting in a $150,000 budget increase and a two-week extension of the planned completion date.

## Question 48
A project manager observed the team's lack of cooperation not long after joining a new company. What steps are most effective in fostering a collaborative work environment?
A. Conducting soft skills development training
B. Opting for a pull-based system for work assignments
C. Organizing team-building activities
D. Adopting an agile work approach

**Question 49**

Regarding the project scope declaration, the following statement are correct, with the exception of:

A. It is an output of the validate scope process.

B. It describes, in detail, the project's deliverables and the work required to create those deliverables.

C. It provides a common understanding of the project scope among project stakeholders.

D. It may contain explicit scope exclusions that can assist in managing stakeholder expectations.

**Question 50**

A project is being led by a contracted project manager who applies a predictive strategy. The project sponsor, who feels that a crucial deliverable has been missed, is not happy with the status of the project thus far. Despite having given their approval to every stage of the project up to this point, they requested that the project manager pause work until they could reevaluate the circumstances. The project manager decided to engage in mediation and arbitration to come to a decision. (Select two)

A. Dispute resolution techniques

B. Coaching techniques

c. Assisted negotiation techniques

D. Direct negotiation techniques

Answer 1 =  B, C and D
**Explanation:**
Hygiene factors and motivational factors serve as the 2 drivers for generating job happiness, based on Herzberg's Motivation Theory model (also known as the Two Factor Theory). Employees are not inspired to work more by hygiene elements; rather, their lack demotivates workers. A clean and safe working environment, income or wage, and job stability are examples of hygiene criteria. Rather than being a hygiene factor, appreciation is thought to be a motivating element.

**Answer  To Question 2 = D**
Explanation: Using the precedence diagramming method (PDM), one can create a schedule model wherein tasks are depicted as nodes & graphically connected through a number of logical relationships to illustrate the order in which they are to be completed.

**Answer  To Question 3= A**
Explanation: The CEO's actions serve as an example of the Halo effect. According to the Halo Effect, decisions are made based on an individual's performance or ability in one particular field. There isn't any real evidence that a team member can oversee a project, except for their technical abilities. The CEO had the notion that each team member could

**Answer  To Question 4= C**
Explanation: Project Cost Management refers to the activities related to planning, estimating, budgeting, finance, funding, managing, and controlling expenses to complete the project within the allocated budget.

Here are the procedures for project cost management:
Determine Budget: This is a process of combining the projected costs of different activities or work units to generate an authorized cost baseline.
Estimate Costs: This is the process of estimating the monetary resources required to execute the task.

Plan cost management.
This is a process of outlining how project costs should be estimated, budgeted for, managed, controlled, and monitored.
Control costs: This is the practice of monitoring the current situation of the project in order to manage changes and update the project costs to the cost baseline.

**Answer To Question  5 = B**
Explanation: To introduce the project, go over expectations, make sure everyone is on board, and address any organizational or personal problems, the project manager should arrange a meeting with the relevant stakeholders. Stakeholder resistance can be addressed by the project manager by simply paying attention to their complaints. To put things in their viewpoint is the goal. To find common ground and determine the cause of such resistance, the project manager needs to comprehend the stakeholder's motivations and driving forces.

**Answer To Question  6 = D**
Explanation: The quality management plan is a part of the process that outlines the tasks and materials required for the project management team to accomplish the quality goals established for the endeavor. It outlines the methods by which relevant rules, regulations, and recommendations will be put

into practice in order to meet quality standards. The quality management strategy can be broad or narrow, formal or informal. The project requirements dictate the specifics and format of the quality management plan. In order to make sure that decisions are founded on reliable information, the quality management plan needs to be reviewed at the beginning of the project. The advantages of this evaluation may include a stronger concentration on the project's value proposition, cost savings, and fewer schedule overruns resulting from rework.

**Answer To Question 7 = A, C, and D**
Explanation: The term "extrinsic motivation" refers to behavior driven by outside forces like money, fame, accolades, or grades. Unlike intrinsic motivation, which originates from within the individual, this type of motivation is derived from outside sources. Giving each team member the freedom to concentrate on projects they are truly passionate about fosters intrinsic drive.

**Answer To Question 8= D**
Explanation: Project Quality Management contains the processes for integrating an organization's quality policies in terms of planning, controlling, and managing projects and product quality criteria in order to achieve stakeholders' objectives. It also assists with regular process improvement actions carried out on behalf of the performing firm.

**Answer To Question 9 = A**
**Explanation:** Finding the reason behind a team member who was once competent but isn't anymore should be the project manager's goal. They should start by identifying the signs, getting in touch with the falling-short team members, having a

conversation with them in order to figure out the problem, offering any assistance they can, tracking and evaluating their progress, and not forgetting to provide feedback.

**Answer To Question 10 = A**
**Explanation:** Just finishing a project on schedule and within budget is insufficient. In order to provide value, you must develop a product that meets the needs of your stakeholders. Ensuring that the individuals who spend money on the final product are satisfied with what they receive is the essence of customer satisfaction. Customer satisfaction is based on the results' usability and conformance to specifications, which let you gauge the extent to which your product lives up to expectations.

**Answer To Question 11: B**
Explanation: The process of acquiring personnel, materials, equipment, facilities, supplies, and other resources required to finish a project is known as acquisition. Periodically, when needed, this process is carried out throughout the project. The main advantage of this procedure is that it provides guidelines and an outline for choosing resources and allocating them to the appropriate tasks. The project's resources may come from sources inside or outside the entity carrying out the initiative. External resources originate by means of procurement processes. Internal resources are obtained (allocated) by functional or resource managers.

**Answer To Question 12 = A**
Explanation: Estimate activity durations using information gathered about the scope of work, skill levels or resource types required, resource calendars, and expected resource quantities. Other variables that could affect the duration estimates are the scheduling network analysis technique employed, the amount of effort put in, the kind of resources (e.g., fixed effort or work, fixed length, fixed number of resources), and constraints imposed on the duration. The member of the project team with the greatest familiarity with the type of work involved in the particular task provides the inputs for the duration estimations. The technique takes into account the availability and quality of the input data and gradually elaborates the duration estimate. For instance, the precision and accuracy of the duration estimations increase with the availability of more exact and detailed data regarding the project engineering and design work.

The duration is unaffected by the particular technique used to analyze it.

**Answer To Question 13 = C**
Explanation: Teams that self-organize typically exhibit higher levels of engagement, ownership, and accountability (PMBOK 7th edition, page 249). Self-organizing teams work without waiting for their managers to give them assignments, in contrast to traditional teams. Rather, kids decide which things need to be completed, rank them, and manage their timetables and due dates independently. On the contrary, a cross-functional team is made up of individuals who possess all the necessary abilities to create a functional product devoid of outside dependencies. Product visibility could only be improved by the product owner via backlog refinement.

**Answer To Question 14 = C**

Explanation: The role of a project manager is a skilled one. She commands the respect of the team due to her PMP certification and advanced level of expertise, which is demonstrated by her years of work in automotive design. Persuasive, formal, and referent power are further types. One's position inside the company determines their formal power. The ability to present reasons that persuade others to act in a certain way is implied by persuasive power.

Referent power occurs when members of the team hold the leader in high regard for personal attributes like brilliance or kindness. Because they tend to appreciate these traits, followers view the leader as an example to follow.

**Answer To Question 15 = B**

Explanation: Information-sharing techniques among project stakeholders can take many different forms. The following variables may influence the communication technology selection:

Information Sensitivity and confidentiality
Project environment
Ease of use
Availability of technology
Urgency of the need for information

**Answer To Question 16 = C**

Change control focuses on finding, recording, and accepting or rejecting modifications to project papers, deliverables, or baselines. Configuration control, on the other hand, is concentrated on specifying both the methods and the outcome.

**Answer To Question 17 = D**
Explanation: The systematic method of monitoring and recording the outcomes of carrying out quality control activities in order to evaluate progress and guarantee that project outputs are accurate, complete, and satisfy client needs.


**Answer To Question 18 = B, C**
Explanation: The project manager can record meetings and distribute the tapes to each participant as a way to resolve the problem. When someone has a question, they can establish a group standard, encouraging people to raise their hands. Additionally, they can make it common practice to raise hands both in in-person meetings and during virtual conferences. The mere fact that attendees frequently forget meeting outcomes does not warrant changing the frequency of meetings. Records and minutes of meetings are useful resources for resolving this kind of problem.


**Answer To Question 19 = A**
Explanation: The following are the inputs for the Plan Communications Management:
Organizational process assets
Enterprise environmental factors
Stakeholder register
Requirements documentation
Project documents
plan Stakeholder engagement plan
Resource management
Project Management Plan
Project charter

**Answer To Question 20 = C**
**Explanation:** Prioritizing stakeholders with high power is emphasized in the PMBOK 7th edition when it comes to stakeholder interaction. Monica and Markus both have a lot of power, but Markus is unaware of it yet, which makes him more dangerous than a powerful but impartial shareholder. The project manager's top goal is to communicate with Markus, exchange project information, and solicit assistance. The second aim is to transfer Monica and Sergio to leadership or supportive roles, with a special emphasis on raising Monica. Sergio is a low-power individual, but attempts must be made to move him away from resistance because power dynamics can change as the project progresses.

**Answer To Question 21 = B**
Explanation: Intelligence does not involve a cultural component because it is an innate mental talent or strength that isn't acquired from individuals or environments.

**Answer To Question 22 = D**
Explanation: Withdrawing is the term used to describe the inability to resolve a problem. This method of resolving conflicts is appropriate when the opposing party is inaccessible or stubborn, or when you need to give the other party a little space to clear their heads or cool off to have a more thorough understanding of the matter (PMBOK 7th edition, page 169). Since the project manager failed to bring up the issue with the sponsor in an attempt to find a solution, the circumstances are not indicative of problem-solving. Because there wasn't any conversation to lessen their differences regarding the sponsor, the project manager did not help to resolve the disagreement either. Documenting the matter, making notes, or capturing information does not constitute a strategy for resolving conflicts.

**Answer To Question 23 = A**

Explanation: Through the establishment of a requirements traceability matrix, each requirement is connected to the project's and business's goals, ensuring that it contributes value to the organization as a whole. A grid known as the requirements traceability matrix connects the original product requirements to the deliverables that meet them. It offers a framework for handling modifications to the scope of the product. In order to guarantee every requirement authorized in the requirements documents are provided at the conclusion of the project, it also offers a way to track requirements throughout the project life cycle.

Among the prerequisites for tracing are, but are not restricted to:

Business needs, objectives, goals, and opportunities;

Product development;

Project scope and WBS deliverables;

Project objectives;

Product design;

High-level requirements plus more detailed ones; and

Test strategy and test scenarios.

**Answer To Question 24 = B**

Define Scope: Outputs

Outputs from the define scope process are as follows:

1. Project document updates 2. Project scope statement:

Stakeholder register

Requirements traceability matrix,

Requirements documentation and

Assumption log.

**Answer To Question 25 = A**

The act of breaking down project work and deliverables into smaller, easier-to-manage components is called "create WBS." The work described in the currently approved project scope statement is represented by the WBS, which also organizes and defines the project's overall scope.

The WBS is a hierarchical breakdown of the whole scope of work that needs to be completed by the project team to meet all project goals and produce the necessary deliverables. This process's primary advantage is that it offers a structure for the deliverables that must be made. This procedure is carried out once or at specific project milestones.


**Answer To Question 26 = A**

Explanation: According to the Expectancy Theory, workers feel that if they put in extra effort, their productivity will increase and they are going to be rewarded, which they value and also encourage them to be more efficient. But if they receive no compensation, like in the scenario mentioned, they are no longer motivated to work hard. According to Theory X, workers are untrustworthy, lazy, and incompetent. Conversely, Theory Y acknowledges that workers are capable, accountable, and trustworthy. The team member is described as compliant; therefore, the circumstances does not fit either Theory X or Y. However, her performance suffered because she did not receive the bonus that she had anticipated. The term "anticipation theory" is imaginary.


**Answer To Question 27 = D**

Explanation: Schedule compression strategies can be employed to reduce or quicken the scheduled timeframe without compromising the project scope for the purpose of fulfilling other schedule objectives, schedule constraints, or authorized

dates. Negative float analysis is a useful method. The path with the least amount of float is the critical path. The entire float may turn negative as a result of breaking a rule or deadline. There are two methods: fast-tracking and crashing.
Crashing: This is a method for adding resources to a timetable to reduce its duration with the least amount of additional cost. Approving over time, adding more staff, or paying to send tasks to critical route activities more quickly are a few instances of crashing. Crashing can result in more risk and/or expense and is not always followed by a workable solution. Crashing only applies to critical path activities where the duration of the activity can be shortened with more resources.

**Answer To Question 28= B**
Explanation: Agile frameworks have a reputation for their transparent and regular communication methods, in which a project manager regularly checks in with his team to see what else could be fulfilled to increase productivity and morale. Everyday standups and everyday communication shouldn't be mixed. The agile team members conduct daily stand-up meetings according to a scrum structure. Depending on the circumstances, your project requires you to employ formal as well as informal communication, regardless of whether you choose to use a predictive or adaptive strategy.


**Answer To Question 29 = C**
The project manager is responsible for giving the new team member the necessary guidance and instruction. According to (PMBOK 7th edition, page 18) Using mentorship and training to enhance a team member's competencies is a starting point when you discover they lack the necessary skills or competencies. Reassigning their work to someone else or doing nothing will not enhance the team member's ability to demonstrate their proficiency; rather, it will cause them to

become demotivated and have a detrimental effect on the project. When all other efforts have failed to get the team members back on track, releasing them should be the last choice.

## Answer To Question 30 = A

Explanation: The project management plan includes a cost management plan that outlines the planning, control, and structuring of the project's expenses. The cost management plan contains documentation on the cost management procedures as well as the related instruments and methods.

## Answer To Question 31 = D

The process of carefully obtaining, evaluating, and interpreting information concerning external opportunities and hazards is known as an environmental scan. PESTEL is an acronym for political, economic, social, technological, environmental, and legal.

The competitor's new product is an illustration of a technology category.

One example of a political category is the banning of goods because of political unrest.

One example of a legal category is the new FDA regulations.

A modification to the project that is related to it is the fourth choice.

Knowledge Area: Business Environment

## Answer to Question 32 = B

Explanation: The scenario suggests collaboration or problem-solving, which results in a win-win situation, considering the project manager decided to meet with the involved team members to address their disagreements and decide on the best option appropriately (PMBOK 7th publication, page 168).

**Answer To Question 33 = D**
Explanation: Data analysis approaches that can be utilized for this process consist of, but don't just apply to cost-benefit analysis.
Every quality action has a cost-benefit analysis that weighs the expected return against the expense of the quality step.
Less rework, more productivity, lower costs, higher stakeholder satisfaction, and increased profitability are the main advantages of satisfying quality standards.
The project manager will be able to assess the cost-effectiveness of the planned quality activities with the use of a cost-benefit analysis.
The optimum option in terms of advantages offered can be found by estimating the strengths and weaknesses of each alternative using a cost-benefit analysis, a financial analysis method.

**Answer To Question 34 = C**
Explanation: It is expected of the project manager to inform stakeholders who have a high level of interest but little authority. He ought to proactively arrange for this set of stakeholders to be informed on a regular basis about the project's status and to follow up with them to ensure they are not having any problems. Furthermore, the project manager can follow up with stakeholders who have considerable interest and power, ensure that stakeholders having low interest and high power are satisfied, and oversee stakeholders who have low power and interest.

**Answer To Question 35 = A**
Explanation: The centralized administration of one or more portfolios in order to accomplish strategic goals is referred to as portfolio management. The main goals of portfolio management are to make sure that initiatives and projects are evaluated in order to determine the best use of resources, and that the portfolio is managed in a way that complements and is consistent with organizational strategies.

**Answer To Question 36 = D**
The project manager wants to take on a leadership role that is more submissive. The following traits, according to the Agile Practice Guide, set servant leadership apart: encouraging self-awareness, listening, supporting teammates, helping individuals develop and grow, using coaching instead of controlling, and encouraging security, trust, and respect. The needs of others are given priority by servant leaders, who enable others to realize their full potential (PMBOK, 7th edition, pages 17–18). Genuine leaders prioritize their own professional development and that of those who follow their personal growth. However, transactional leaders use rewards and punishments as tools for motivation. They concentrate on supervision, organizing, and performance. In addition to fostering an environment of creativity and innovation, transformational leaders prioritize inspiring others.

**Answer To Question 37 = B**
Explanation: Schedule compression strategies can be employed to reduce or quicken the scheduled timeframe without compromising the project scope for the purpose of fulfilling other schedule objectives, schedule constraints, or authorized dates. Negative float analysis is a useful method. The path with the least amount of float is the critical path. The entire float

may turn negative as a result of breaking a rule or deadline. There are two methods: fast tracking and crashing.

Fast tracking. A schedule compression approach in which ordinarily sequential activities or phases are executed in parallel for at least some of their time. Building a building's foundation before finishing all of the architectural designs is one example. Only when it is possible to overlap tasks in order to reduce the project's critical path duration does fast tracking become effective. Rapid tracking could lead to more risk and redo. When a timeline is accelerated, using leads typically results in more work being done to coordinate the various processes and raises the chance of quality issues. Project expenses may also rise as a result of fast tracking.


**Answer To Question 38 = D**

Explanation: Team storming is what the project manager's group is going through. The most challenging and important phase a team may experience is storming. Forming, storming, norming, performing, and adjourning are the five steps identified by Tuckman's team development ladder (PMBOK 7th edition, page 166). This stage sees the emergence of distinct personalities, which leads to rivalry and conflict. The team's performance will now suffer greatly as a result of their energies being diverted into fights and arguments.


**Answer To Question 39 = D**

Project complexity arises from human behavior, organizational behavior, and uncertainty in the organization itself and its surroundings. The following is a definition of the three complexity dimensions:

Uncertainty: uncertainty about new problems as well as ignorance or perplexity.

Systemic actions: the interconnectedness of parts and systems.

Human actions: the interaction of many people and groups.

[Knowledge Area: Project Scope Management, Monitoring, Domain: Process]

**Answer To Question 40 = A**
Explanation: Parametric estimating comprises the examination of cost, programmatic, and technological data to locate cost drivers and construct cost models across every phase of the project's cost as well as duration parameters.

**Answer To Question 41 = B.**
The traits of servant leadership are empathy, stewardship, and listening. You must first determine what is unclear or the reason for the team member's lack of comprehension of the assignment before moving further.

Knowledge Area: Business Environment
**Answer To Question 42 = C**
Explanation: One of the most crucial features of the Agile methodology is flexibility, as the work scope can adjust to accommodate new requirements. Regularly gathering stakeholder feedback is encouraged by agile, change-driven, or adaptive approaches. A Change Control Board (CCB) is not used in the Agile strategy, in contrast to the predictive approach.

**Answer To Question 43 = D**
A range of tools are used to maintain and disseminate project information, including:
Project management tools: Web-based interfaces for scheduled and managing projects software, tools for collaborative work, software for virtual offices and meetings, and other project management applications;
Electronic communications management includes phone, voicemail, fax, email, video and web conferencing, web publishing, and web pages.

Electronic hard-copy document management includes memoranda, reports, press releases, letters, and email.

**Answer To Question 44 = A**

Explanation: The source of legitimate power, also known as formal, positional, or authoritative, is an individual's position or formal title. Given that there isn't any evidence of their using other types of authority in the scenario at hand, the project manager's superiors' choice is based only on their position. However, expert power is dependent on the belief held by subordinates that the leader possesses a high degree of expertise or a particular set of talents that set them apart from others. Referent power is the capacity of a leader to sway followers by inspiring respect, admiration, or a sense of identity with them. Conversely, situational power refers to earning respect and gratitude for stepping up to save the team or the project in a particular circumstance.

**Answer To Question 45= B**

Explanation: Organizations can use one of numerous PMO structure types, each with a different level of control and influence over projects. Examples of these include the following:

Directive: Through direct project management, PMOs seize control of the projects. The PMO provides a great level of control.

Controlling: PMOs in charge enforce compliance and offer assistance in a variety of ways. Compliance can include introducing project management frameworks or methods, applying specified templates, forms, and tools, or sticking to governance. The PMO offers a decent amount of control.

Supportive: Supportive PMOs offer training, templates, information access, best practices, and lessons from previous projects, all of which help projects in a consultative capacity. A PMO of this kind acts as a repository for projects. There is little control offered by the PMO.

**Answer To Question 46 = B**
Explanation: Under transformational leadership, a project manager encourages the team by supporting their ideas and fostering an environment that fosters creativity and innovation. Conversely, laissez-faire leaders take a hands-off approach, completely trusting and depending on the team to establish their own guidelines and reach judgments.
The combination of transactional and transformational leadership is known as interactional leadership. On the other hand, a transactional leader, who bases their team management on the authority to reward and punish, supports policies and processes.

**Answer To Question 47 = D**
Explanation: Because Option A includes an expansion to the project's scope that has been accepted by the customer, a $150,000 budget increase, and a two-week extension of the anticipated completion date, it is the most reasonable reason for "re-baslining" the project. When it comes to project management, it's important to consider a baseline whenever there is a major change in the project scope, schedule, or budget.
In this particular case, the client has clearly approved an extension of the project's scope, which in all indications is a convincing argument for changing the baseline. Option A is a legitimate and acceptable reason for re-basing the project since the budget increase and schedule extension are directly related to the authorized scope modification.

**Answer To Question 48 = C**
Explanation: When team-building exercises are regularly conducted during the course of a project, especially in its early

phases when relationships between team members are still developing, they promote a cooperative working environment. Choosing a pull-based job assignment system, such as the lean or Kanban method, is more about increasing productivity and cutting down on delivery times than it is about encouraging teamwork. Soft-skills training may help your team communicate and work together more effectively, but it is not as successful as team-building exercises. Furthermore, adopting an agile methodology shouldn't be done merely to foster better teamwork because the project might not be a good fit for it in the first place.

**Answer To Question 49 = A**
Explanation:
Project Scope Statement
The project scope, key deliverables, presumptions, and constraints are all described in the project scope statement. The project deliverables are fully described in the project scope statement. The project and product scopes are included in the documentation of the whole scope. Explicit scope exclusions may be included, which can help control stakeholder expectations. It also gives project stakeholders shared knowledge of the project's scope. It offers the starting point for determining whether requests for alterations or extra work fall inside or outside the parameters of the project. It helps the project team plan more thoroughly and provides direction for the team's work as it is being carried out. The following are included in the full project scope statement, either directly or by references to other documents:
Project exclusions. Determine what is not included in the project; making this clear to stakeholders can help control expectations and prevent scope creep.
Acceptance criteria. a list of requirements that must be fulfilled for deliverables to be approved.
Deliverables. Any distinct and verifiable output, outcome, or

capacity to carry out a service must be generated in order to finish a process, stage, or project. Ancillary results like project management reports and documentation are also included in the deliverables. These deliverables might be explained in great depth or in short form.

Product scope description gradually expands on the features of the good, service, or outcome that are outlined in the requirements documentation and project charter.

**Answer To Question 50 = A, C**

Explanation: Both arbitration and mediation entail using a mediator or an arbiter to help parties come to an agreement. Indirect or assisted negotiation techniques, such as arbitration or mediation, should be taken into consideration when direct negotiation is unable to yield a satisfying outcome. When a mediator works honestly to reduce differences, an arbitrator looks at the legal aspects of a disagreement. Another means of resolving disputes is litigation, which involves taking the matter to court as a final resort when all other avenues have been exhausted. Arbitration and mediation do not qualify as coaching practices; instead, they are employed to assist others in becoming more productive and efficient in the workplace by setting an example, offering praise, constructive criticism, and so on.

## Question 1
The relative importance of the risks that have been identified for a project must be determined. Which of the following jobs has the highest chance of having no bearing on this order of importance?
A. Researching the stakeholder register
B. Making a review of the assumption log
C. Generating the risk report
D. Examining the risk register

## Question 2
The leadership of the company wishes to see more agile approaches used in their projects. What should be done at first in a project before implementing any agile approaches?
A. Examine the organization's culture and readiness for transformation
B. Conduct an employee survey to identify those who are willing to take part in agile projects
C. Provide agile training to the members of the team that was put together for the pilot project
D. Put ongoing work on hold while you restructure it to fit the new agile cadence

## Question 3
Every day, numerous individuals and specialized teams from the construction project are present at the job site. To guarantee safe and effective advancement, the team leads must communicate with each other on a regular and smooth basis. Which agile procedure can this project implement to improve timely cross-functional
A. Retrospectives
B. Daily standups

C. Iteration reviews
D. Risk-based spikes

## Question 4
Pairs of members of your project team are writing code and evaluating each other's efforts to see if the code complies with the requirements documents. Which of the following outcomes will this method produce?
A. Work performance data
B. Verified deliverable
C. Accepted deliverable
D. Acceptance criteria

## Question 5
Two risk replies are being considered by the project team for inclusion in the risk register. The initial risk response is $5,000 and needs to fulfill two requirements. Only $2,000 is needed for the second risk response, which needs to fulfill four requirements. Which course of action is the project team least likely to adopt to decide on the appropriate risk response?
A. Conduct a cost-benefit analysis
B. Use multicriteria decision analysis
C. Run a Monte Carlo simulation
D. Perform an alternative analysis

## Question 6
An assembly line construction project is almost finished. In addition to closing procurements, submitting the final project report, and updating the lessons learned register, the project manager also gathered input from pertinent stakeholders. What action should the project manager take next?
A. Send a summary of how the final product fulfilled the business needs
B. Transfer the completed assembly line to operations
C. Send formal written notice to the vendors, notifying them

that the contracts have been completed
D. Make the final payment to the suppliers

## Question 7
You work on a project team that is creating a brand new class of automobiles. You are about to begin working on a collection of duties (the work package) related to the vehicle's braking system. Before starting work, you would like to evaluate the acceptance criteria. How would you go about getting this information?
A. Requirements documentation
B. The WBS dictionary
C. Project management plan
D. Activity attributes

## Question 8
As the project manager, you oversee a group of developers who are employed in rented office space to develop software. The code is taking longer to write than expected. You've asked the landlord to extend the office's lease by one more week. Sadly, you have been informed by the landlord that the office is reserved for that time. The project materials contain a description of the issue. What ought you to do next?
A. Makes updates in the risk register
B. Request more funds
C. Enter the issue in the issue log for the record
D. Make revisions to the resource management plan

**Question 9**

A project is implemented to lower the manufacturing process's fault rate. The project team is analyzing and refining the process through quality assurance efforts. For this project, which of these options would be most advantageous?
A. Utilizing rolling wave planning for the project
B. incorporating a kanban board into the production process
C. Adopting a just-in-time (JIT) manufacturing process
D. Getting professional advice from a Six Sigma Black Belt certified consultants

**Question 10**

As part of developing a communications management plan for a construction project, you want to assess the information needs of the project stakeholders. Your attention is on the kind and arrangement of information that you must convey to them. Which is the best thing for you to do?
A. Conduct a communication requirements analysis
B. Consult the stakeholder engagement plan
C. Develop the stakeholder register
D. Review the requirements documentation

**Question 11**

You are in charge of managing a product development project that makes use of an agile framework. In order to address risk, criteria for success, and other relevant issues, you wish to gather SMEs and stakeholders together. What is the most effective strategy for you to achieve this?
A. Lead a retrospective of the iterations
B. Do interviews with the people you've identified.
C. Schedule a focus group
D. Call the appropriate individuals for the daily scrum meetings

## Question 12

An organization's project management office (PMO) makes sure that all project management procedures and pertinent project documentation follow accepted best practices. When identifying stakeholders for a new project, what should the project manager look at first?

A. The stakeholder engagement plan to identify what management strategies and actions can work best to effectively engage the stakeholders

B. The business documents to obtain information about the stakeholders

C. The requirements documentation to know more about potential stakeholders

D. The communications management plan to learn about the project's stakeholders

## Question 13

In a project divided into four phases in sequence, what should the project manager do when the second phase is over and the third one is about to begin?

A. Begin the process of directing and managing the project work

B. Start the process of monitoring and controlling the project work

C. Perform the process of identifying the project stakeholders

D. Begin the process of developing the project management plan

## Question 14

You wish to hire a new contractor to complete the identical task because the current one is not meeting your expectations for performance. It is your responsibility to ascertain the precise legal process involved in contract termination early. How should you proceed?

A. Check the procurement management plan
B. Review the risk register
C. Consult the contract
D. Look at the scope statement

## Question 15

A business establishes a change control board (CCB) with the specific goal of examining and rating all project modifications. Out of the following, which one best sums up a person or organization that has the authority to seek modifications to a project when the sponsor of the project is a member of the CCB?

A. Project sponsor
B. Project team
C. Project manager
D. Any stakeholder

## Question 16

The team and project are carrying out the process of monitoring and controlling project activity within the scope of a process improvement project for a factory running. Which of these events occur throughout this process?

A. Drawing an actual comparison of project performance against the project management plan
B. Gaining formal acceptance of the deliverables by the customer or sponsor
C. putting accepted changes requests into practice to accomplish the project's goals
D. evaluating change requests and making the decision to accept or reject them

## Question 17

You discover a missing component in a project's requirements management strategy when looking over it. Which one of these is the strange one?

A. A procedure outlining the method for ranking the project's requirements

B. How will requirements activities be scheduled, monitored, and reported?

C. The metrics that will be used and the rationale for using them

D. A procedure outlining the steps involved in creating a project scope statement

## Question 18

Pam, one of your top programmers, was recently elevated to team leader of the agile development process. Pam was an excellent software programmer, and you assumed that her promotion would allow her to impart her knowledge to the other members of the development team. However, you see that Pam doesn't live up to your expectations and gives a lackluster performance in her new role. Which empirical guideline did you overlook or forget when thinking about Pam's promotion?

A. Pareto concept

B. Murphy's law

C. Expectancy Theory

D. Halo effect

## Question 19
While tracking the baseline cost of a project, it is discovered that the project expenses are greater than projected at this time. What is the most plausible explanation for this?
A. An incomplete milestone list
B. Overestimated material costs
C. Lack of stakeholder support
D. Excess inventory


## Question 20
Development is an important part of a large-scale project involving regulatory and environmental contemplation. When it comes to preliminary project planning, what should be your first move?
A. Start identifying stakeholders for the purpose of engaging them as a requirement for project planning
B. Organize a project kick-off meeting with the stakeholders for the purpose of informing and engaging them and obtaining commitment
C. Analyze the project charter to get noteworthy information concerning the project
D. Share project scope with the involved team to establish a uniform agreement on the deliverables of the project

## Question 21
The project sponsor requests a copy of the file which comprises the description, source, owner, priority, and position of product requirements. What is he asking of?
A. The scope management plan
B. The requirements management plan
C. The requirements traceability matrix
D. The work break-down structure (WBS)

## Question 22
Which of the following is not an output of the closing process?
A. The final product, service, or result of the project
B. A lessons learned knowledge base
C. Organizational closure documents
D. The project management plan


## Question 23
While overseeing a software upgrade project for your organization, you notice that your sponsor has high decision-making authority but little interest. What stakeholder management technique should you use to keep the sponsor's support?
A. Manage the sponsor closely
B. Keep the sponsor satisfied
C. Keep the sponsor informed
D. Monitor the sponsor's actions


## Question 24
A project's goal is to study the technical, economic, and social viability of building a hydroelectric dam. The project sponsor approves the project charter. What is the next step to be taken?
A. Identify Risks
B. Develop Project Management Plan
C. Develop Project Charter
D. Identify Stakeholders'

## Question 25

You are responsible project that entails the construction of 5 bridges. The project is grouped into 5 phases, each of which completes one bridge. After the first stage of the project is concluded, which process group from the 2nd phase should be used?

A. Executing
B. Closing
C. Initiating
D. Planning

## Question 26

A corporation is considering two projects: Alla and Bella. Alla's net profit is expected to be $60 million, while Bella's is predicted to be $55 million. BThe two initiatives are rewarding and pleasing, but the corporation can not invest in but of the but have to choose one of them. Calculate the opportunity cost if Alla is chosen.

A. $55 million
B. $95 million
C. $10 million
D. $60 million

## Question 27

Which of the following is not an input to the controlling process?

A. The project management plan
B. The project schedule
C. The project work
D. The approved changes

## Question 28

All the following are input to the developing project management plan process except one?
A. Project charter
B. Stakeholder register
C. The enterprise's environmental factors
D. The organizational processes and procedures

## Question 29

What is the output of the monitoring and controlling process?
A. The project schedule
B. The project charter
C. The project management plan
D. The project work

## Question 30

Which of the following is not a process group?
A. Initiation
B. Planning
C. Execution
D. Closing

## Question 31

When a control chart is used, outliers are
A. A common result of rare random causes that are hard to verify or replicate
B. Insignificant outputs, measurement mistakes that don't require further investigation
C. Singular quantifications beyond the bandwidth of a lower and upper control limit.
D. Inconsistent measurements, with seven results above or below the mean value.

## Question 32

In which process of risk management is it decided to transfer risks?

A. Plan risk response
B. Identify risks
C. Monitor and control risks
D. Perform quantitative risk analysis

## Question 33

As a project manager, you see conflicts occurring within a team on both interpersonal and technical levels. What is the best way to handle this issue professionally and appropriately?

A. Conflict is bad for smooth operation which reduces productivity. As soon as problems emerge, resolve them.
B. Immediately resolve disputes in private. Adopt a straightforward and cooperative strategy.
C. In order for everyone to work together to develop a solution, bring up the problem during a team meeting.
D. Focus on accomplishing your objectives and use your ability to coerce others to settle disputes swiftly.

## Question 34

A project manager is calculating the risk of her project. Several of her experts are not on-site but would like to be included. How will you deal with this?

A. Use the Delphi technique
B. Use the critical path methodology
C. Use the Monte Carlo analysis with the internet as your tool
D. Evaluate options for corrective action that is recommended

## Question 35

It is getting harder to calculate the precise risk-cost impact. As a project manager, it should be evaluated based on

A. A quantitative basis
B. A qualitative basis
C. An economic basis
D. A numerical basis


## Question 36

Consider yourself the project manager in charge of establishing and engineering several business processes as well as one customer relationship management (CRM) software solution. This project involves multiple organizations, including a huge firm and numerous suppliers. As time goes on, you can see the impact of different corporate cultures. There are various businesses as well as process expectations regarding the manner in which the project will be handled, resulting in several misunderstandings among stakeholders. There is also lack of trust issue and rising skepticism. What will you do first to bring these disparate set of stakeholders together?

A. Allow the issues to get worse until they become out of control before raising an escalation.
B. Examine the implications and likelihood of every scenario's risks. Before you react, prepare a course of action.
C. Rather than letting little things divert your attention, concentrate on the task at hand.
D. Implement a collaborative quality policy that demands agreement from all project-participating organizations.

## Question 37
Risk tolerance is calculated to aid
A. The project manager in estimating the project.
B. The management knows how other managers are going to execute the project.
C. The team is ranking project risks.
D. The team in scheduling the project and deadlines.

## Question 38
What is your best option as a project manager, when you want estimate the duration of an activity:
A. Consult the experts whose job will do what is needed to obtain precise estimates.
B. Make your best estimation about the duration of each task because deadlines are subject to change as the project progresses and additional data is gathered.
C. Make a rough estimate of what your budget will allow and add extra.
D. None of the above.

## Question 39
The following factors are vital for the process of risk management, except:
A. Lessons learned
B. Project status reports
C. Historical information
D. Work breakdown structure

## Question 40

Consider the possibility of an earthquake causing harm to your construction project. The contractor informs you that the contractual terms cannot be met due to a specific contract clause. What is the name of this clause?

A. Fixed price clause
B. Force majeure clause
C. Contract obligation
D. None of these

## Question 41

If you find a 90% chance of any risk event occurring, with the result being $10,000, what is represented by $9000?

A. Present value
B. Contingency budget
C. Risk value
D. Expected monetary value

## Question 42

At a bidding convention, you run across a dear friend of yours who is a bidder. How do you proceed from here?

A. As a demonstration of trust, reveal some personal details.
B. Let your management team know about the relationship
C. Find a way to discontinue with bidding process
D. You have to make him understand that you are honest by refusing him the contract

## Question 43

As a project manager, you regularly meet with the team to review lessons from earlier projects. What's the name of this activity?

A. Scope identification

B. Performance management
C. Project team status management
D. Risk identification

## Question 44
Which of the following statement is correct?
A. A program represents a tiny part of a larger project
B. A program is made up of several related projects
C. A program is a combination of different unrelated projects
D. None of the above

## Question 45
Which word best describes RACI mean?
A. Recommend, Accountability, Consulted, Inform
B. Responsible, Accountable, Consulted, Inform
C. Response, Accounting, Consulted, Inform
D. Responsible, Accounting, Confirm, Inform

## Question 46
Which step of the risk management strategy allows you to identify risk?
A. Identified Risks and Control and Monitor Risks
B. Track Identified Risks
C. Perform Quantitative Risk Analysis to Identify Risks
D. Performed Qualitative Risk Analysis to Monitor and Control Risks

## Question 47
The deadline for the undertaken project is approaching. However, as a competent project manager, you have only recently realized that only 75% of the project's scope is already fulfilled. You submit a change request. In your change request, what authorization are you requesting?

A. Increasing approval for the use of contingency financing
B. A longer period to complete the schedule.
C. Extra resources are available through the contingency fund.
D. Corrective action depends on situational causes.

## Question 48

How likely is it that a risk is going to occur in the project's fourth month if its anticipated duration is five months and there is a 20% probability that it would occur in one month?
A. 80%
B. 20%
C, 60%
D. Less than 1%

## Question 49

There is a 60% probability that a project will make $100,000 and a 40% chance that it won't. What is the project's expected monetary?
A. $100,000 profit
B. $60,000 loss
C. $ 20,000 profit
G. $40,000 loss

## Question 50

Mandi works as a project manager in a pharmaceutical firm. She has been given a new innovative project and is deciding which project life cycle she will utilize. Which choice should she select from the list below?
A. Agile
B. Hybrid
C. Iterative

D. Predictive

Answer To Question 1 = C

Answer To Question 2 = A: Evaluate the organizational culture and transformation readiness

**Explanation:**
How to Evaluate Organizational Culture in 4 Steps
1. A value assessment
A values assessment is crucial for organizations to evaluate if they are actively living their values. It should evaluate employees' and leadership's actions against desired behavior, incorporating values into annual reviews.

2. Consider cross-functional metrics
Regularly evaluating cross-functional data helps identify trends and impact the organization's culture.

3. Gather employee input
One effective method for assessing company culture is by checking in with the employees through surveys. While pulse surveys are quick and simple for workers to complete, engagement surveys evaluate the happiness and health of employees. Organizations can continuously assess their culture and take appropriate action when these strategies are balanced. For continuous assessment, determining a survey's approach and frequency is essential.

4. Review external indicators

Evaluation of organizational culture necessitates consideration of honors and accolades from the company as well as other sources such as Indeed and Glassdoor. Employees can share their candid opinions in these anonymous forums, which can highlight problems and have an impact on hiring and retention. Good organizational culture assessment creates joyful, healthy, and long-lasting work environments.

Answer To Question 3 = B

Daily stand-ups refer to daily short meetings attended by the project team and relevant stakeholders to discuss the progress of the project. It is usually done while standing because of the short duration of time the meeting will last.

Answer To Question 4 = B
Verified Deliverable

Answer To Question 5 = C
Answer: Run a Monte Carlo simulation

Explanation: A mathematical method for predicting the potential outcomes of an unknown event is the Monte Carlo simulation. When there is a chance of random variables, a Monte Carlo simulation is a model used to estimate the likelihood of various outcomes. The influence of risk and uncertainty on prediction and forecasting models is better understood through the use of Monte Carlo simulations.

Answer To Question 6 = B

Answer To Question 7 = B
Explanation: The details of the tasks, activities, progress, and comprehensive details in the work breakdown layout are found in a WBS glossary. The project scope, any relevant progress, and, in certain cases, the cost, dates, resources, value, and quantity are all included in the content.

**Answer To Question 8 = D**
Explanation:
Project Revision is a methodical and impartial evaluation of a project's potential to succeed based on its specific needs and circumstances. It is necessary for you to employ project management techniques and processes, including resource allocation, managing tasks, managing issues, handling changes, and communication management. It is imperative that you make certain the change is executed in compliance with the revised plan, quality standards, and stakeholder expectations. Finding regions with greater risk or improvement potential is the aim of the analysis. A suggested action plan and other recommendations are included in the analysis.

Answer To Question 9 = D
Explanation: The Six Sigma certification is a mark of proficiency and knowledge in the Six Sigma project management methodology. Although the PMP is a general certificate for project managers in many industries, the Six Sigma certification is unique to this manufacturing process management system.

Answer To Question 10 = A

Explanation: One technique for figuring out what information the stakeholders require is communication requirement analysis. It can be gathered through interviews, workshops, and even by reviewing the lessons learned from past initiatives. This makes it possible for project managers to better regulate the flow of information, which improves communication planning.

Answer To Question 11 = C

Explanation: Focus groups are organized interviews consisting of three or more individuals, usually up to twelve. The moderator guides the participants in discussing a certain topic, starting from a general point of view and gradually narrowing it down to a more concentrated one. It's a means of gathering ideas by using representatives of a bigger population.

Answer To Question 12 = B

Answer: The business documents are used to obtain information about the stakeholders.

Answer To Question 13 = C

Answer: Perform the process of identifying the project stakeholders.

Answer To Question 14 = C

Answer: Consult the contract
Answer To Question 15 = D
Answer To Question 16 = A

Explanation: As per the Project Management Body of Knowledge (PMBOK® Guide), project control is defined as a project management function that entails assessing actual performance against planned performance and implementing suitable corrective measures (or advising others to take such measures) to achieve the intended result.

Answer To Question 17 = D

Answer To Question 18 = D

Explanation: According to the Halo Effect, decisions are made based on an individual's performance or ability in one particular field. There isn't any real evidence that Pam can oversee a project, except for her technical abilities.

Answer To Question 19 = D
Explanation: Excess inventory is any inventory that exceeds planned demand. It typically implies some form of stock demand mismanagement owing to a variety of factors such as erroneous demand planning, unforeseen weather changes, canceled orders, seasonality, holidays, or viral consumer trends.

Answer To Question 20: C

Answer To Question 21 = C
Explanation: The Requirements Traceability Matrix (RTM) is a tool or document that assists project managers in establishing and tracking the progress of their projects. It aids in delivery monitoring by giving a digital thread regarding each demand from the start to the finish of the project.

Answer To Question 22 = D

Answer To Question 23 = B
Explanation: To receive continuous support from the sponsor, the stakeholder management strategy to adopt is an active engagement and communication-focused stakeholder management strategy. which involves keeping the sponsor satisfied through:
Regular Communication
Stakeholder Meetings
Status Reports
Issue Resolution
Relationship Building
Celebrating Success
Feedback Mechanism



Answer To Question 24 = D
Answer: Identify Stakeholders

Explanation: Following the creation and approval of the project charter, the process of identifying stakeholders begins.

Answer To Question 25 = C

Explanation: The first stage in launching a new project is project initiation. During the project initiation phase, you determine why you're conducting the project and what business value it will provide, and then utilize that information to gain support from key stakeholders. Initiating. A new project or new phase of an existing project is defined by the initiating process Group.

Answer To Question 26 = A

Explanation: $45 million. Opportunity Cost = Net Profit of Beta. The value of the alternative not chosen is called the the the the the the opportunity cost which is the predicted net profit of Beta.

Answer To Question 27 = A

Explanation: The input to the controlling process is the project management plan.


Answer To Question 28 = B

Explanation: The stakeholder registry is an input to the process of building a project management plan.

Answer To Question 29 = C
Answer To Question 30 = D

Answer: Closing is not a process group.
Answer To Question 31 = C
Answer To Question 32 = A

Answer To Question 33 = B

Address conflicts from the start privately. Use a collaborative and direct approach.


Answer To Question 34 = A

Explanation: Use the Delphi method. It is generally used to obtain expert opinions on technical issues, project scope, and so on.

Answer To Question 35 = B

Answer To Question 36 = B

Answer To Question 37 = C

Answer To Question 38 = A

Answer To Question 39 = B
Explanation: Typically, project status reports are not available the very first-time risk management is conducted. As a result, not every time is it employed as an input for risk management.

Answer To Question 40 = B
Explanation: This situation is a Force majeure clause which is a contract condition that releases both parties from liability if an extraordinary occurrence immediately stops one or both parties from executing.

Answer To Question 41= D
Explanation: The concept of Expected Monetary Value (EMV) is
a decision-making method that helps to assess the probable effect of a decision and gives a cost price to each eventuality. It's a method of calculating the expected loss or gain from a project based on the likelihood of various outcomes.

Answer To Question 42= B
Explanation: Since there is a conflict of interest, the ideal thing to do is inform your management team of this relationship to avoid conflicts of interest and adhere to principles of ethical conduct in project management.

Answer To Question 43 = B
Explanation: Project performance management refers to the process where you develop and organize projects that increase the organization's performance and objectives. It looks at the wider picture of how a project helps a company achieve strategic success. The question talks about refreshers on lessons from past projects, which can help project managers keep track and evaluate the of carrying on with a project and also monitor their efficiency and alignment with defined business goals and objectives.

Answer To Question 44 = B
A program consists of several related projects.

Answer To Question 45 = B

Answer To Question 46 = C

Answer To Question 47 = D
Action for correction based on situational causes

Answer To Question 48 = B

Answer To Question 49= C. $ 20,000 profit
Explanation: The formula for calculating Expected Monitory Value (EMV) is EMV = Probability × Impact.
After calculating the positive and negative values, sum them:

$100,000 \times 0.6 = \$60,000$. $\$40,000 \times \$100,000 = 0.4$ EMV less $\$40,000$ equals a $\$20,000$ profit.

Answer To Question 50 = A

www.ingramcontent.com/pod-product-compliance
Lightning Source LLC
Chambersburg PA
CBHW050452290526
45786CB00006B/2267